TRAINING YOUR SUPERPUPPY

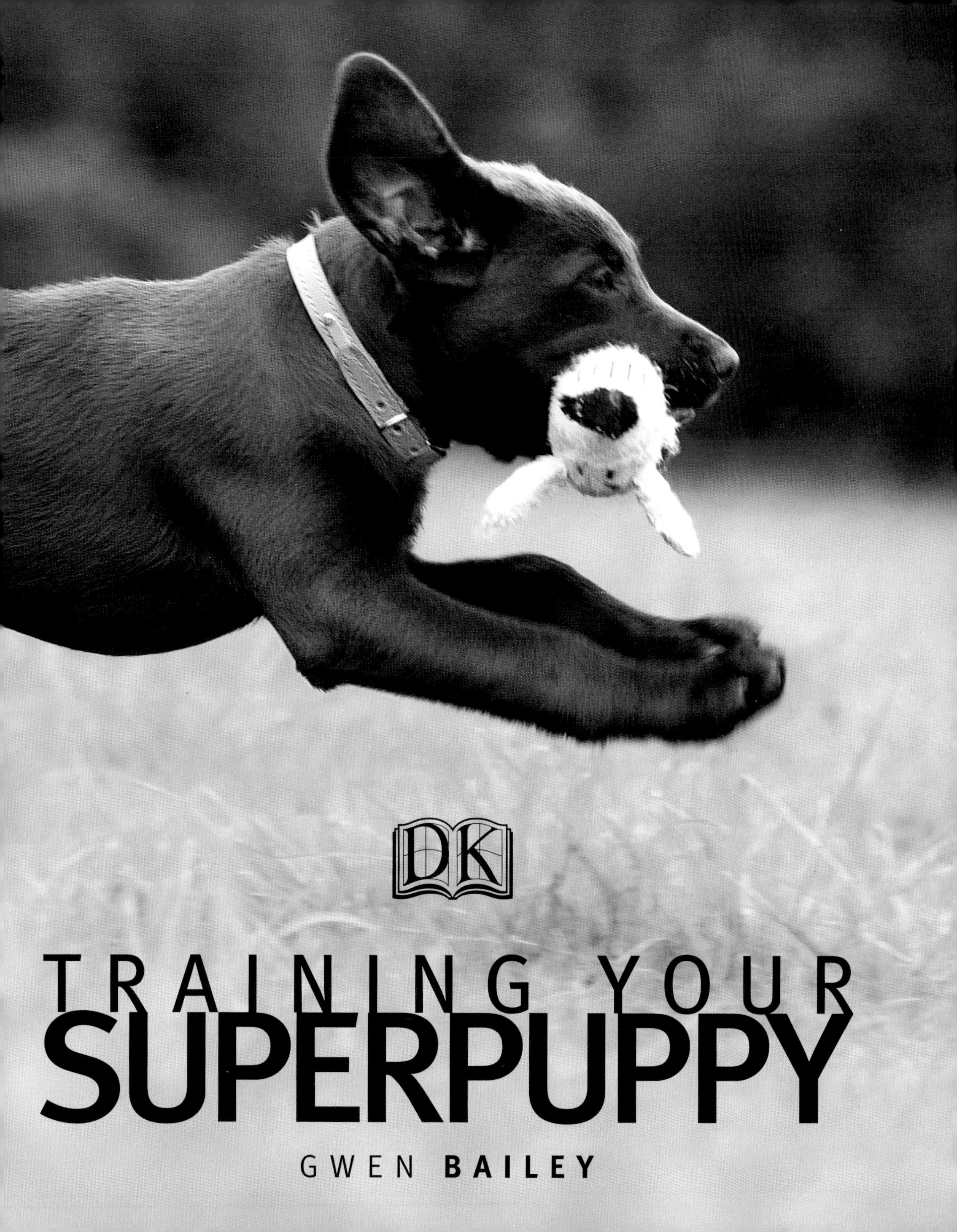

TRAINING YOUR SUPERPUPPY

GWEN **BAILEY**

LONDON, NEW YORK, MELBOURNE,
MUNICH, AND DELHI

DORLING KINDERSLEY
Project Editor Victoria Wiggins
US Editor Shannon Beatty
Senior Art Editor Vicky Short
Project Art Editor Amy Orsborne
Designer Philip Fitzgerald
Design Assistant Victoria Foster
Jacket Designer Silke Springies
Production Editor Joanna Byrne
Production Controller Emma Sparks
Photographer Gerard Brown
Art Direction Nigel Wright, XAB Design
Managing Editor Camilla Hallinan
Managing Art Editor Karen Self
Art Director Phil Ormerod
Associate Publisher Liz Wheeler
Publisher Jonathan Metcalf

DK INDIA
Editorial Manager Rohan Sinha
Senior Editor Ankush Saikia
Editor Sreshtha Bhattacharya
Design Manager Arunesh Talapatra
Senior Designers Sudakshina Basu, Mitun Banerjee
Designers Shriya Parameswaran, Arijit Ganguly, Niyati Gosain, Payal Rosalind Malik, Nidhi Mehra, Pallavi Narain, Arushi Nayar, Pooja Verma
Production Manager Pankaj Sharma
DTP Manager Balwant Singh
Senior DTP Designers Dheeraj Arora, Jagtar Singh
DTP Designer Bimlesh Tiwary

Published in the United States by
DK Publishing, 375 Hudson Street, New York, New York 10014

11 12 13 14 15 10 9 8 7 6 5 4 3 2 1
001—180014—08/2011

Published in Great Britain by Dorling Kindersley Limited.

A catalog record for this book is available from the Library of Congress.
ISBN 978-0-7566-7180-8

Printed and bound in Singapore by Tien Wah Press

Discover more at
www.dk.com

Contents

△ **Time of discovery**
Young puppies spend much of their time investigating and playing, creating a wealth of experiences to help them handle new things in the future.

▽ **Meeting children**
Socializing with children of all ages, from toddlers to teenagers, is important for puppies if they are to develop into friendly adult dogs.

△ **Positive training**
Training with rewards will help your puppy to learn what you are asking him to do. It will also increase his trust and respect.

Introduction

Puppyhood is a lovely time, full of promise and joyful energy. It is also a time of great learning and needs to be an active journey of discovery and education if a puppy is to grow and develop into a well-adjusted dog.

Raising a puppy is similar to raising a child, but it all happens much more quickly. Fully grown by 1 year old, a puppy develops rapidly. It is easy to miss critical stages of their education (especially if you have work commitments or a busy social calendar) unless you are well prepared and know what to do. This book will help you teach all that is necessary to ensure your puppy learns essential lessons at the appropriate time.

I'm often asked to list the most important ways for a puppy owner to raise a puppy well. It's difficult to choose, but my favorite few are to socialize well, train early using positive methods, reward often, have fun, build a good relationship, and, when things go wrong, find positive solutions that work for both you and your puppy. The ideas contained within this book will help you to approach these aspects of puppy ownership with confidence.

▽ **Just rewards**
Avoiding scolding and punishment and instead rewarding the correct behavior will result in a well-trained dog and a good relationship.

△ **Focused on fun**
Using toys to teach your puppy to enjoy playing games with humans will build a strong bond, and will be fun for both of you.

▽ **Mutual affection**
A relationship based on love and trust will give you the best foundation on which to raise a contented, well-behaved dog.

There is no denying that puppies are adorable, but with each of them comes a responsibility for their future well-being and happiness. Get it right in their first year and you set them up for a lifetime of contentment as a successful pet. Get it wrong and they face an uncertain future, full of recriminations for bad behavior which is not their fault. Getting it right isn't difficult if you put in the effort, but you need to know exactly what to do. This book gives you that knowledge and gets you off on the right foot and paw for a wonderful life together. I wish you luck and success.

Gwen Bailey is an internationally renowned behavorist and trainer. She lectures worldwide, is the author of many best-selling books on dog behavior, including DK's *Training Your Superdog*, and is a long-standing member of the UK's Association of Pet Behaviour Counsellors. Gwen worked for an animal welfare charity in the UK for 12 years as Head of Animal Behavior. During this time, she helped rehabilitate thousands of rescue dogs and put them on the path to good behavior. To do more preventative work, she set up Puppy School, which provides a network of positive training classes for young puppies in the UK.

1

The **right puppy** for **you**

Choosing a puppy

Finding the right puppy to suit you and your family is really important. The **genes** your puppy has **inherited** and **where he comes from** will have a huge impact on his future happiness and behavior. A **puppy** that has a **good start in life** will **fit readily into your home,** and can be brought up to be a **contented, well-behaved dog**. In contrast, a puppy from a bad breeder will be difficult to raise, with all sorts of physical and mental problems. This section explains how to **choose your puppy wisely**. By putting **time, effort, and thought** into what type of puppy to get and where to get it from, you will have a **solid foundation** for your **superpuppy**.

RAW MATERIAL
All puppies are different—each has a unique combination of genes and experience that shapes its future behavior and temperament.

Choosing the right puppy

What type of dog will make the best pet for you and your family? Decide what you want before buying and you will avoid future disappointment in your pet's behavior and characteristics.

Size, shape, and traits

Generations of selective breeding have created a wide range of dogs with different appearances and temperaments. Before you go out to look at puppies, you need to do a lot of research and make many decisions. Only in this way are you sure find a puppy that has the traits, body shape and size, and personality to fit your lifestyle.

Sit down with your family and discuss what you want from a dog. How much time do you have? Do you prefer big or small, hairy or non-shedding, delicate or robust? Some decisions carry penalties. A non-shedding coat may mean you will have to pay for professional grooming throughout your dog's lifetime. Choose a long-haired, silky breed and you will need to carry out grooming sessions every day yourself. Are you willing to make that kind of commitment?

As well as physical characteristics, consider carefully what traits your future dog should have. Should he be bold or hesitant, companionable or aloof? Researching what a breed was bred for provides clues to a dog's behavior and what he likes to do (pp.20–1). Talking to owners will give you some ideas about how these traits work within families.

Energy and exercise

Think about your own character. Are you an extrovert who would enjoy the exuberance of a Boxer, or are you a quiet type who would prefer something more reserved, like a Whippet? Asking such questions will help you find a dog that suits your temperament, so that you fit easily together without personality clashes.

Getting energy levels right is important, too. Many breeds were bred to work, so they have the stamina to keep going all day. If you don't have much energy and would prefer a dog to lie down and do nothing most of the time, then a working breed is not for you.

Find out how much exercise your choice of dog will need. One of the best ways to do this is to ask other people who own the breed that interests you. People who live with these dogs can give you useful insights into both the benefits and downsides of your chosen breed. Doing this research before viewing puppies will allow you to consider other breeds that may be a better match for your needs.

△ **Companion puppy**
Many owners enjoy their dog so much, they decide to get another one, bringing greater companionship for them and their other dog.

◁ **Family dog**
It is often better to wait until your children are of school age before getting a puppy, so that you have more time available for his upbringing.

Born to run
If you are very active, buying a puppy that will grow into a dog that enjoys exercise will increase the time you spend together and bring pleasure for you both.

Where to **find your puppy**

There are many sources of puppies: some very good, some not so good, and some that are really bad. Finding a healthy puppy that has been well reared by a caring breeder will give you both a good start.

The right breeder

Once you have decided on the type of dog you want, your next step is to find a healthy puppy with a good temperament. This is harder than it sounds. Finding breeders is easy, but finding good ones—and telling the good from bad—is not.

▽ **Rescue pup**
Dog rescue homes and shelters often have whole litters, or single, older puppies, both pure- and cross-bred, that are in need of a good home and will grow up to make excellent pets.

One of the first things to consider is why breeders have litters to sell. Do they breed working dogs or show dogs, or did they breed a much-loved pet in order to have another similar pet? Was it all an accident or did they breed simply to make money? Apart from the last two, all these reasons have merit, but find out whether a breeder has taken the puppies' future temperament and health into account, and not put either aside in pursuit of other goals.

To find a good breeder, you will need to do a lot of research. Ask owners of adult dogs you like where their dog came from, and go to dog shows, asking as many people as possible for recommendations.

Pedigree health tests

Health testing is important when it comes to pedigree (pure-bred) dogs. Many breeds are created from small gene pools and interbreeding, which has resulted in numerous genetic diseases and defects. Some of these can be tested for, and it is vital to research your chosen breed to assess what problems it, and you, may have to face in later life. Find out what tests should be done, and

Pet stores

Steer clear of puppy mills, that breed solely for money. Their puppies are often delivered to your door, or "warehoused" in pet shops or puppy outlets where several breeds are housed together for convenience. Some try to pass themselves off as home breeders. Be suspicious if the mother is not with her litter, and avoid puppy warehouses completely.

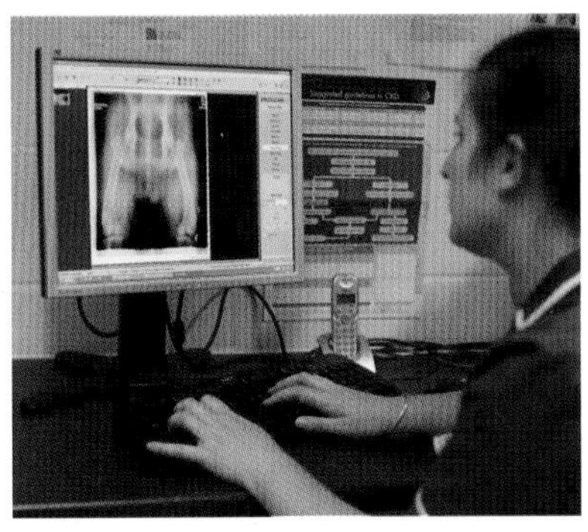

△ **Health issues**
Pedigree dogs are at risk for many inherited diseases and conditions that need to be tested for. Prospective owners should be aware of what these are before buying a pedigree puppy.

◁ **Show dogs**
Some unscrupulous breeders are solely interested in winning prizes—with no concern for heath or temperament—and sell off their surplus stock to unsuspecting puppy owners.

what any test scores may mean. Ask to see paperwork for both parents, and even the grandparents, of any litter. Be very suspicious if this is unavailable, and find another breeder who is more willing to answer questions.

The right environment

It is extremely important to find breeders who raise litters in a home environment (pp 16–17) rather than in kennels away from the house. Breeders to avoid run "puppy mills," that breed purely for financial gain without considering the welfare or future health and temperament of the offspring. The mother of the litter may be hidden from view, and these dogs are often kept outside in appalling conditions.

One good source of puppies is owners who have bred from a pet dog—provided they have thought carefully about both parents' health and temperament. Ask them about this before going to view the puppies. Some rescue shelters may also be a good source of healthy puppies, as long as the puppies have been well handled and properly assessed.

▽ **Difficult choice**
It is up to you to choose a healthy puppy of sound temperament. You can only do so if you are fully aware of the facts.

Choosing a **good breeder**

A puppy's early life with his breeder has a big effect on future behavior. Establishing good habits and socializing a puppy well will have a lasting impact, so it is important to choose a breeder carefully.

The first weeks with the breeder have a huge impact on a puppy's development. A good breeder will already have considered a dog's health and temperament before breeding, and makes sure puppies are healthy and well socialized by the time they go to a new home.

When you visit a breeder, check that the puppies are raised indoors, so that they are used to the sights and sounds of everyday life. Look for evidence that they spend time in the house, such as toys, water bowls, and bedding, and observe them as they move around the home and garden. Are they cautious or do they run around exploring? Watch how they react to household noises. A puppy that jumps when the phone rings or a door slams is not used to being in a home environment.

◁ **Careful breeder**
A good breeder will make the effort to socialize the puppies with many different people and other animals, as well as getting them used to a wide range of sights, sounds, smells, and situations.

Socialization skills

Probably the most important thing a breeder can do for a puppy is to socialize it with people of all ages. Ask for details about how this has been done, especially with men and children. Watch carefully to see how the puppies react. A well-adjusted

"A puppy that will **happily approach** you is one that is **socialized and well adjusted."**

Δ **Advance training**
Well-raised puppies that have been encouraged by their breeder to go to the bathroom outside from an early age will soon learn good habits.

◁ **Well bred**
Conscientious breeders will produce healthy puppies from healthy parents. They will also keep them at a good weight, and free of worms and fleas.

puppy approaches happily, climbing up to get closer to your face. A puppy that flattens itself and is reluctant to come toward you may not have been socialized properly or at all.

If the mother is not kept with the litter, find out why. Ask to see her and check her temperament and overall health. Her genes have been passed on to her puppies.

Early housebreaking

Observe what bathroom procedure is in place for the puppies. Is there enough room for them all to sleep in the nest, and are they able to move to a clean area to relieve themselves? Does the breeder take them outside regularly after sleeping, eating, and playing? If so, housebreaking will be easy. If conditions are dirty, or there is no distinction between nest and toilet, housebreaking will be difficult.

Good breeders should spend lots of time watching the puppies and will know their individual personalities. If they do, be guided by them as to which one might be best for your home. But choosing an individual puppy from a litter is less important than choosing a good breeder who has done everything correctly. Be prepared to walk away and find another breeder unless everything has been done well.

▽ Happy with humans
One of the most important things a breeder must do is ensure that the puppies meet and have positive encounters with a wide range of people as early in life as possible.

Nervous mothers

If a mother is worried about people, she will pass on her fears to her puppies, through her genes and her behavior. Even though it may be hard to walk away from a litter, puppies bred from nervous mothers are best avoided since they can make difficult pets.

Popular dog breeds

When you are **choosing a dog**, think about the **needs** and **characteristics** of many breeds before narrowing down your search. Different breeds have **widely contrasting personalities** and **physiques**, so find one that **fits in** with your **lifestyle**. This section profiles the **most popular** dog **breeds**. Each entry describes a different breed, outlining **individual characteristics** and **personality traits**, as well as **grooming and exercise requirements**. Pick your favorite breeds from among these and continue your **research** to make sure your new pet is **right for you**.

LIVELY OR LANGUID? Choosing a breed to suit your family and lifestyle is essential if you want your puppy to grow up to be the dog you dreamed of.

The **breed catalog**

Looking at the history of a breed and how and why it was developed can tell you a lot about what traits your new puppy is likely to have. It will also give you an idea of what characteristics and personality to expect.

Dog breeds can be divided into six main groups, listed below. This division provides a general idea of how these breeds were developed, and what traits were selected for.

To start with, find out about each breed from the descriptions that follow (pp.22–49). Books, the Internet, and talking to experts on the breed can all help you to understand what the dog you want to own may be like, what its strengths and weaknesses are, and how its characteristics will fit in with your family and lifestyle. All this information will assist you in choosing the right puppy, as well as help you make the most of his traits. You will also learn how to channel his natural desires—for example, chasing—into productive activities.

Dogs to help hunters

Gun dogs were bred to help hunters flush game from its cover and retrieve it once shot. They generally have high energy levels, but are extremely willing to please. Gun dogs make great pets for active families who have plenty of time to give their pets the exercise and attention they need to be contented. They enjoy playing and are easily trained.

German Shorthaired Pointer

Dogs to kill vermin

Terriers and ratters were bred to catch and kill small animals. They are active, bright, and feisty, with plenty of character, and are quick to act in their own defense, if necessary. They enjoy games with squeaky toys and are not safe around small pets.

Border Terrier

Dogs to help shepherds

Shepherd dogs were bred to help herd sheep and cattle. They have a highly developed chase instinct and are sensitive and loyal, with a strong desire to work and exercise. These dogs are good for energetic families. Another group, the flock guardians, were bred to live with sheep and keep predators away.

Shetland Sheepdog

Companion dogs

Bred for generations to be pets, true companion dogs are usually small in size and have gentle, sociable natures. Surprisingly, only a few of these breeds were bred solely for companionship; most were originally selected as watchdogs or for other specific purposes.

Shih Tzu

Dogs to hunt

A variety of dog breeds were bred to track and catch different animals. They can be divided into those that hunt by sight, and those that follow scent trails. Hunting dogs have a strong pack instinct and an intense desire to chase moving animals. Although they are sociable, they are more independent and less willing to please than many other breeds.

Basset Hound

Other working dogs

Many dogs were bred to fulfill a variety of roles: anything from guarding homes and property to pulling small carts or rescuing people lost in the snow. These dogs come in many different shapes, sizes, and temperaments, depending on the type of work they were designed to do.

Doberman Pinscher

Active gun dog
Springer Spaniels were bred to work tirelessly all day, every day. As a result, they have an incredible energy that can be difficult to use up in a family home.

Small dogs

Small dogs fit into small places and can be taken anywhere easily. They are less intimidating than bigger dogs and cost less to maintain, although they need just as much attention.

◁ **Fun-loving**
Shih Tzus may be small, but they are energetic and fun-loving too, and need many play sessions, especially when they are puppies.

Most of the smaller breeds of dog have small bodies and big personalities. Many of them do not think of themselves as small and are ready and willing to take on a world that is much larger than themselves.

Small dogs are compact and are therefore ideal for people who do not have much living space. They are less likely to bowl people over, but can trip them up by getting under their feet. Small dogs can be carried and are put into a bag or a carrier for safe and easy passage on public transportation. Although they are commonly known as "toys," small dogs are all dog and need as much care as their larger cousins. Many of the smaller breeds, however, require less exercise than large dogs, and so are more suited to people living in urban areas or those who have more sedentary lifestyles.

◁ **Intimidating world**
Little dogs such as Chihuahuas live in a world of giants, and need plenty of reassurance that things around them are safe.

Chihuahua

Size *2–7lb (1–3kg), 6–9in (15–23cm)*
Character *Feisty, lively, loyal*
Exercise *Minimal*
Grooming *Minimal*

Chihuahuas are the smallest of all dogs and come in long-haired and short-haired varieties. Puppies of this breed are tiny and delicate, and great care must be taken to keep them safe. Chihuahuas will do best in gentle, careful homes where their owners can gradually introduce them to life among giants.

△ **Adult**
Chihuahuas are often shy unless socialized and protected from bad experiences as puppies.

Vulnerable, bulbous eyes

Yorkshire Terrier

Size *6–8lb (2.5–3.5kg), 9in (23–24cm)*
Character *Lively, feisty, courageous*
Exercise *Minimal to moderate*
Grooming *Daily grooming and regular clipping*

Yorkshire Terrier puppies are lively and sensitive. They need careful socialization and handling when young. Bred in the 19th century to kill rats, Yorkshire Terriers have a feisty nature, which can emerge if they are threatened. Their non-shed coat needs daily grooming and hair around the eyes needs to be clipped or tied up so they can see where they are going.

Long, silky coat needs daily grooming

◁ **Adult**
Yorkshire Terriers are active, playful, and intelligent—they will quickly learn new exercises with training.

Maltese

Size *4–7lb (2–3kg), 8–10in (20–25cm)*
Character *Friendly, fun-loving, playful*
Exercise *Minimal*
Grooming *Daily grooming and regular clipping*

Maltese puppies are sweet, full of fun, and sociable. They can take time to learn to be clean indoors, but they make up for this inconvenience by being friendly and loving. An ancient breed from the island of Malta, for many generations the Maltese has been bred as a companion dog. The result is a happy little dog that makes an ideal pet for owners who enjoy spending time caring for their long hair. Gentle, slow acclimatization to grooming is needed during puppyhood, together with regular visits to the groomer throughout life. The hair on their head should be clipped or tied to enable them to see out.

Soft and silky white fur

◁ **Adult**
The long hair on the head is traditionally tied back from the face so that Maltese dogs can see where they are going.

Toy Poodle

Size *6–9lb (2.5–4kg), 10–11in (25–28cm)*
Character *Intelligent, good-natured, lively*
Exercise *Moderate*
Grooming *Daily grooming and regular clipping*

Toy Poodles are gentle, sweet, and calm. The puppies are lively, agile, and quick to learn, and will rapidly return any investment you make in terms of training. The Toy Poodle is the smallest of the poodles, bred from the Standard Poodle, whose original function was as a duck retriever. They are social dogs and thrive best in a careful household where there is plenty of stimulation. During puppyhood, they need to be carefully introduced to the grooming and clipping procedures that will keep their coats in good condition in later life. Their ears are hairy inside and you will gently need to familiarize them with having the hairs plucked from an early age to keep the ear canals open and clean.

△ **Smart and thoughtful**
Despite their small size, Toy Poodles may surprise their owners with their intelligence and thoughtful way of working things out.

△ **Adult**
Poodles come in a variety of colors, including cream, blue, red, and black. This adult has been given a "puppy show clip."

Pomeranian

Size *4–6lb (2–2.5kg), 9–11in (22–28cm)*
Character *Active, intelligent, good watchdog*
Exercise *Minimal to moderate*
Grooming *Extensive daily grooming*

Pomeranians are miniature versions of sled dogs from Greenland and Lapland. Puppies of this breed are lively and extroverted. They can be noisy when excited, and barking should be discouraged to prevent a bad habit from forming. Start grooming and brushing early in puppyhood to keep their profuse coats in good condition.

△ **Adult**
Pomeranians have a very thick coat with a warm undercoat and can get too hot in heated houses.

Miniature Pinscher

Size *8–10lb (3.5–4.5kg), 10–12in (25–30cm)*
Character *Active, protective, intelligent*
Exercise *Moderate*
Grooming *Minimal*

Puppies of this breed are very small and delicate and great care needs to be taken to protect them from boisterous children or large pets. Due to their feisty nature, Miniature Pinschers need good socialization throughout puppyhood. Give them plenty to do to keep them busy and stimulated.

Distinctive tan and black markings

◁ **Adult**
Miniature Pinschers were first bred in the 19th century to kill rats on farms in Germany.

Havanese

Size *7–13lb (3–6kg), 8–11in (20–28cm)*
Character *Playful, good-natured, sociable*
Exercise *Minimal to moderate*
Grooming *Daily grooming and regular clipping*

The Havanese has a happy, friendly temperament. Puppies are sweet, active, and eager to please, although they can be difficult to housebreak. Clip or tie hair back from their eyes so they can see out, and accustom them to gentle grooming early to help them relax while their silky fur is being managed.

Hair clipped on the face to give good visibility

△ **Adult**
A Havanese's silky coat needs daily care to prevent tangles, along with regular visits to the groomer for clipping.

Bichon Frise

Size *7–13lb (3–6kg), 9–12in (23–30cm)*
Character *Playful, good-natured, sociable*
Exercise *Minimal to moderate*
Grooming *Daily grooming and regular clipping*

Sweet-natured and friendly, the Bichon Frise makes an ideal pet. Puppies are active and lovable, although owners will need patience when it comes to lessons and housebreaking. Tie up hair away from their eyes so they can see clearly, and get them used to grooming early so that coat care is easier when they are older.

△ **Adult**
The Bichon Frise was first developed on the island of Tenerife, and has been a favorite for centuries in France and Spain.

Shih Tzu

Size *11–15lb (5–7kg), 10–11in (25–27cm)*
Character *Intelligent, independent, alert*
Exercise *Moderate*
Grooming *Daily grooming and occasional clipping*

Shih Tzu puppies are cute and appealing. However, their strong character means that early socialization and training are vital if you are to prevent bad behavior later. Start gentle grooming early to make coat care easy, and tie hair away from eyes so they can see to socialize. Unfortunately, their shortened faces, exaggerated by breeders, can lead to breathing difficulties and distress when overheated.

Shortened face can create breathing problems

◁ **Adult**
These alert, intelligent dogs were originally bred by Tibetan monks and Chinese emperors.

△ **Ready for action**
Puppies are lively and need active, playful owners who will help use up their energy in a positive way.

Miniature Poodle

Size *10–18lb (4.5–8kg), 11–15in (28–38cm)*
Character *Intelligent, agile, good-natured*
Exercise *Moderate*
Grooming *Daily grooming and regular clipping*

The Miniature Poodle is the middle-sized poodle. Slightly more robust than the Toy Poodle, and much smaller than the Standard Poodle, Miniature Poodles are lively, active, and endearing as well as fast learners. They are calm when they need to be and are rarely clumsy or careless. Poodle comes from the German word *pudel*, meaning to splash in water, and the Poodle's ancestors were bred in the 15th century for hunting water birds. Miniature Poodles are smart and agile, and were once famed for their performances in circuses. Nowadays, they are popular among agility and obedience competitors and make smart, energetic workers. The Poodle's pom-poms were once thought necessary to protect joints from cold water, but most pet poodles have a "pet clip," which is one length all over. Make grooming sessions fun and gently accustom your puppy to the feel of clippers from an early age, so that coat care is an easy task.

Non-shed fur is soft and fluffy

△ **Adult**
Regular visits to the groomer and daily coat care are needed to keep a poodle's soft, curly coat in good condition.

Papillon

Size *9–10lb (4–4.5kg), 8–11in (20–28cm)*
Character *Intelligent, lively, sensitive*
Exercise *Moderate*
Grooming *Daily*

Called the "butterfly dog" because of the shape of its large, hairy ears, the Papillon is lively, playful, and dainty. Papillons are inclined to be sensitive, and careful socialization is needed to ensure they grow up to be well adjusted. They are loyal and devoted to trusted owners, but can be a little aloof and indifferent to strangers. They are intelligent and easily learn lessons, such as how to be clean in the house.

△ **Adult**
Adults have feathery ears in the shape of butterfly wings, which is where the breed gets its name from.

Boston Terrier

Size *10–25lb (4.5–11.5kg), 11–17in (28–43cm)*
Character *Gentle, good-natured, enthusiastic*
Exercise *Minimal to moderate*
Grooming *Minimal*

Boston Terrier puppies are skittish and inquisitive, although they are easily worn out. Smaller than the similar-looking French Bulldog, they have retained little of the true, predatory terrier nature and are sweet-natured, sociable, and easygoing. Their low exercise requirements make them ideal for urban life, but their shortened noses can lead to snoring, as well as breathing problems during exertion.

△ **Adult**
Owners are attracted to the human-like expressions on a Boston Terrier's shortened face.

Lhasa Apso

Size *3–15lb (6–7kg), 10–11in (25–28cm)*
Character *Alert, active, vocal*
Exercise *Moderate*
Grooming *Extensive daily grooming*

Lhasa Apso puppies are funny and full of character. As adults, they are strong-willed and intelligent, so need good socialization and training while young. Originally bred in Tibet to be watchdogs for monasteries and temples, Lhasa Apsos need to be discouraged from barking when young to prevent it from becoming a bad habit.

△ **Adult**
Adult Lhasa Apsos can bark excessively—a sign of their watchdog origins—so early training is needed.

Growing hair needs daily grooming

Parson Russell Terrier

Size *11–18lb (5–8kg), 11–15in (28–38cm)*
Character *Feisty, active, tenacious*
Exercise *High*
Grooming *Minimal*

The Parson Russell Terrier is recognized by kennel clubs and holds a true pedigree. Puppies of this breed are lively, active, and inquisitive to the point of getting into trouble or danger unless they are watched carefully. Adults are predatory around small animals and need early socialization and training to prevent problems later in life.

◁ **Adult**
Parson Russell Terriers were created in the 19th century to run with hounds and flush out foxes.

Border Terrier

Size *11–15lb (5–7kg), 10–11in (25–28cm)*
Character *Friendly, active, docile*
Exercise *Moderate*
Grooming *Minimal plus periodic stripping*

Although once bred in the Scottish Borders to kill foxes and rodents, many Border Terriers have now lost a lot of their true terrier nature and make good pets. Puppies are active and curious, but can also be thoughtful and careful. Adults can be feisty if challenged and so need early socialization with other animals if they are to be good with them in later life. When mature, Border Terriers have the stamina and energy to keep going all day, but are also happy to rest and adapt their exercise levels to those of their owners. They are very adaptable and, if well socialized, can be taken anywhere, their small size allowing them to be carried on public transportation or car journeys. They are easy to train and have a happy, fun-loving disposition that makes them undemanding to live with.

△ **Adult**
Stripping the old topcoat produces a smooth outline. As the topcoat grows, Border Terriers develop a more shaggy appearance.

△ **Excellent companion**
Border Terriers make great pets, since they are affectionate, resilient, and intelligent. Their cheerful nature also makes them good family dogs.

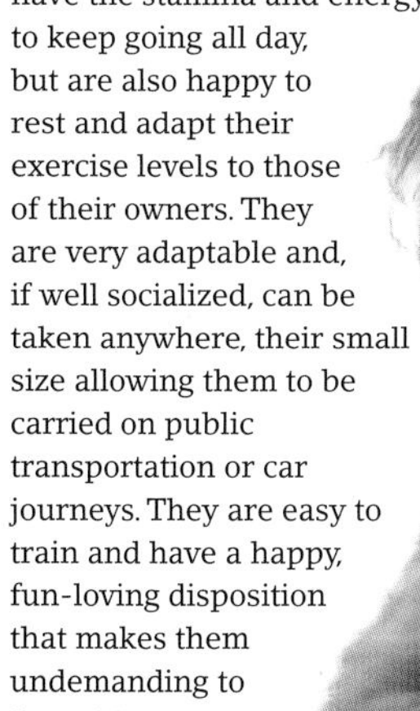

Coat will need regular stripping—removal of the topcoat by a groomer—when mature

Cairn Terrier

Size *13–15lb (6–7kg), 10–12in (25–30cm)*
Character *Active, playful, sociable*
Exercise *Moderate*
Grooming *Minimal plus periodic stripping*

Cairn Terriers like to be busy and thrive in a stimulating environment. As puppies, they are lively and inquisitive. When adults, they can be predatory, having been bred in the 17th century to hunt foxes, rats, and rabbits around the cairns (rock piles) in Scotland, so early socialization with cats and other animals is recommended. It is not advisable to trust them with small pets.

△ **Adult**
A Cairn Terrier's wiry coat needs to be stripped by a groomer twice a year to remove the old, loose hair of the long topcoat.

Wiry coat does not shed much hair

Cavalier King Charles Spaniel

Size *11–18lb (5–8kg), 12–13in (31–33cm)*
Character *Friendly, sweet-natured, playful*
Exercise *Moderate*
Grooming *Daily*

Cavalier King Charles Spaniels are the epitome of a companion dog, being sweet-natured, happy, and easygoing. As puppies, these spaniels are adorable, easily trained, and fit well into most households. With a less flattened face than the King Charles Spaniel, which is a different breed, the Cavalier King Charles Spaniel has a longer nose and a flatter skull. Sadly, inherited diseases abound within the small gene pool for this breed, making it difficult to find a litter with disease-free genetics.

Bulbous eyes are a typical feature

△ Adult
Cavaliers are true pets, having been bred since the 16th century to be companions. They come in many colors, including tricolor and black and tan.

Pug

Size *13–18lb (6–8kg), 10–11in (25–28cm)*
Character *Friendly, outgoing, good-natured*
Exercise *Minimal*
Grooming *Minimal*

Pug puppies are appealing, full of character, and quick to learn. Modern-day Pugs have a very small gene pool, which leads to inherited health problems. The shortened nose can cause breathing difficulties and snoring. Despite this, they are popular because of their expressive faces, good nature, and happy disposition.

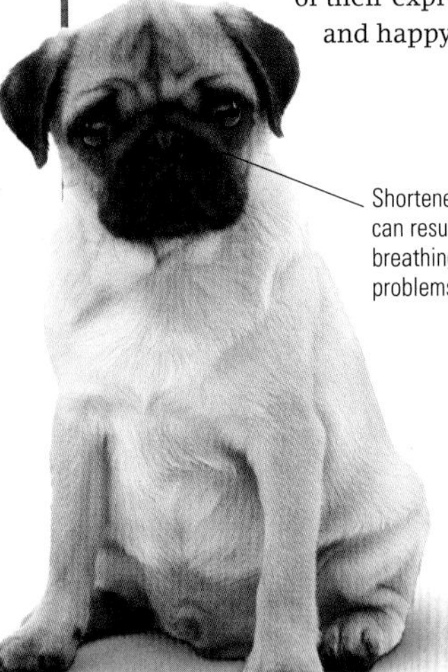

Shortened nose can result in breathing problems

△ Adult
Pugs are thought to have been bred originally in China. Due to their small gene pool, all Pugs are very similar to one another.

West Highland White Terrier

Size *15–22lb (7–10kg), 10–11in (25–28cm)*
Character *Feisty, active, vocal*
Exercise *Moderate*
Grooming *Daily grooming and regular clipping*

West Highland White Terriers are feisty and full of life. Barking should be discouraged early and lots of socialization is needed. Puppies are sweet, but training needs to begin early if owners are to keep control later. Because West Highland White Terriers are naturally predatory, they are often unreliable around small pets. Skin conditions abound, so be careful to choose from healthy stock.

◁ Adult
West Highland Terriers are lively and inquisitive, and prone to barking at intruders and all slight disturbances as well as with excitement.

Dachshund

Size *15–32lb (7–14.5kg), 10–11in (26–28cm)*
Character *Placid, playful, easygoing*
Exercise *Moderate*
Grooming *Minimal*

Dachshunds come in two sizes, miniature and standard, and in three coat types. They often suffer from bad backs due to their shape, and slipped disks are common. Care should be taken to support the spine when lifting them up, and rough play with other dogs and children should be discouraged. Dachshunds are happy, laid-back, and fairly independent in character.

Smooth-haired Dachshund

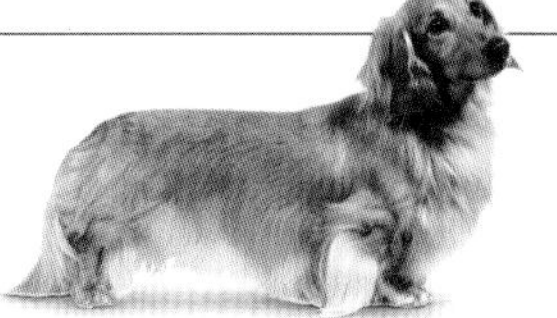

Long-haired Dachshund

Long back can result in slipped disks

Wire-haired Dachshund

△ **Adult**
Dachshunds come in three coat types, smooth-haired, long-haired, and wire-haired, none of which is high maintenance. They also come in a variety of colors.

Miniature Schnauzer

Size *13–18lb (6–8kg), 12–14in (30–36cm)*
Character *Lively, playful, sociable*
Exercise *Moderate*
Grooming *Daily grooming plus regular clipping*

Miniature Schnauzer puppies are sweet and playful, and make good pets for families if well socialized with children. Originally bred as watchdogs and to control vermin on farms, these dogs will warn of intruders, though excessive barking needs to be controlled while young. They may also be unsafe with small pets and need good socialization with cats. They are intelligent and learn lessons easily if you are clear and fast with your teaching. Daily coat care is essential, along with regular visits to the groomers, so begin acclimatization to grooming and handling early.

△ **Bright and lively**
Miniature Schnauzers are a high-spirited breed. Channeling their inquisitiveness into activities with you will stop them from getting into mischief elsewhere.

△ **Adult**
Adults are energetic yet dainty, never clumsy. Their small size makes them ideal for compact homes.

Long hair around the mouth needs careful cleaning

Medium dogs

Medium-sized dogs are suitable for people who would like a large dog but do not have room. These dogs are less delicate than small dogs and so are better suited for families with children.

Medium-sized dogs are easier to handle than large dogs, but have more of a presence than small dogs. Although they still need plenty of free running and walks, most medium-sized dogs do not require quite as much time spent on exercise as larger breeds. In addition, they need less food and usually have lower veterinary insurance premiums. They also fit into small spaces, so suit a compact lifestyle and can be happy living in urban areas. Medium-sized dogs are usually robust enough to play with children and other dogs, and are less easily injured than smaller breeds. They are too big to be stepped on or injured accidently and won't get under your feet in the way that tiny dogs often can. They are easier for children to manage than bigger dogs, do less damage if they get boisterous, and are less likely to pull you over if you are not strong. They also create less mess than their larger canine cousins.

◁ **Strong-willed**
Cocker Spaniel puppies have a strong nature and need confident owners to take control.

△ **Family dogs**
Medium-sized dogs, such as this Tibetan Terrier, are more resilient than small dogs. They won't knock children over as easily as large dogs can.

Shetland Sheepdog

Size *13–15lb (6–7kg), 14–15in (35–37cm)*
Character *Timid, gentle, sensitive*
Exercise *Moderate*
Grooming *Extensive daily grooming*

Shetland Sheepdogs are shy and delicate, and best suited to owners who are gentle, careful, and kind. As puppies, they need lots of outings and socialization to gain confidence. They are playful and loyal to trusted owners, but they are also prone to worrying, so they do best with easygoing, relaxed owners.

◁ **Adult**
Shetland Sheepdogs were originally bred in the 17th century to herd livestock in the Shetland Islands, Scotland.

French Bulldog

Size *22–28lb (10–12.5kg), 12in (30–31cm)*
Character *Affectionate, outgoing, good-natured*
Exercise *Minimal*
Grooming *Minimal*

Puppies of this breed are inquisitive and full of fun. They love to be the center of attention and their extroverted nature will keep onlookers entertained. French Bulldogs make excellent pets, having been bred since the 19th century to be companions. They bark only when necessary. They like to be clean and may try to avoid getting dirty. They thrive best with happy owners who have strong characters. Their flattened faces can cause snoring and breathing problems, and can make them prone to overheating on a hot day.

◁ **Adult**
Adults have strong, compact bodies that are heavy for their small size, and a gentle, fun-loving character.

Tibetan Terrier

Size *18–30lb (8–13.5kg), 14–16in (36–41cm)*
Character *Intelligent, vocal, enthusiastic*
Exercise *Moderate*
Grooming *Daily grooming and regular clipping*

These dogs were once bred as watchdogs by monks in Tibet. They are lively, but barking needs to be discouraged and puppies need lots of socialization while young. Accustom them to grooming early so they get used to the extensive brushing needed to keep their long coats in good condition.

◁ **Adult**
Adults have long, silky hair and so time is needed every day to groom the coat and remove tangles.

Staffordshire Bull Terrier

Size *24–37lb (11–17kg), 14–16in (36–41cm)*
Character *Enthusiastic, playful, energetic*
Exercise *High*
Grooming *Minimal*

Staffordshire Bull Terrier puppies are friendly and playful, but they have a hard bite. As adults, they are usually good with humans, especially children, but due to being bred originally for dog fighting, they can be problematic with other dogs unless properly socialized from a very young age. Staffordshire Bull Terriers suit a busy, active family.

△ **Adult**
Feisty and strong, adults can pull surprisingly hard for their size and so careful training is needed.

Fox Terrier

Size *15–18lb (7–8kg), 15–16in (39–40cm)*
Character *Feisty, lively, impulsive*
Exercise *Moderate to high*
Grooming *Minimal*

There are two breeds of Fox Terrier, the Smooth and the Wire. Both are feisty, active, and playful, and both originated from hunting dogs used to unearth foxes. They are easily excited and will be predatory around small pets. Puppies need to be very well socialized, especially with other dogs, to prevent issues from developing later.

△ **Adult**
Fox Terriers make elegant-looking pets for those who can handle their feisty nature.

Corgi

Size *24–37lb (11–17kg), 11–13in (27–32cm)*
Character *Intelligent, protective, loyal*
Exercise *Moderate*
Grooming *Minimal*

There are two breeds of Corgi, the Pembroke Welsh and the Cardigan. Both were bred to drive cattle, and all puppies of these breeds need careful socialization and training to overcome their natural reserve. Corgis are playful dogs, and benefit from active owners.

△ **Adult**
Corgis' tendency to nip at heels, which used to help them drive cattle, needs to be controlled from an early age.

Beagle

Size *18–31lb (8–14kg), 13–16in (33–40cm)*
Character *Sociable, independent, vocal*
Exercise *Moderate to high*
Grooming *Minimal*

Beagle puppies are very endearing. Good training is needed for puppies since these dogs were originally bred to hunt hares and rabbits, and the drive to follow scents and chase is strong. Beagles have a happy hound temperament, so make lovely pets if you can handle the control problems on walks.

◁ **Adult**
Beagles are sociable and easygoing, and get along well with humans and other dogs.

Lovable rogue
Staffordshire Bull Terrier puppies are inquisitive and always ready to get into mischief. They make good pets if they are treated kindly and are well socialized with other dogs from an early age.

Whippet

Size *28–30lb (12.5–13.5kg), 17–20in (43–50cm)*
Character *Gentle, calm, affectionate*
Exercise *Moderate*
Grooming *Moderate*

Known as the "poor man's greyhound," the Whippet was developed in the mid-19th century for hunting rabbits and other small game. As puppies, Whippets are lively but delicate, and may need protection from the excesses of rough play with children and boisterous dogs. They are gentle creatures and can be timid, so careful, caring owners suit them best. They are calm and affectionate at home, but they can have control issues on walks, since they have a tendency to take off after things that move fast. Due to their thin coats, they will need protection from cold weather.

Slender legs can be fragile

△ Adult
Whippets are prone to feeling the cold, but they also need protection from scratches since their skin is easily torn by thorns.

Brittany

Size *29–33lb (13–15kg), 19–20in (47–50cm)*
Character *Intelligent, active, eager*
Exercise *High*
Grooming *Extensive daily grooming*

Brittanys are good working dogs and need plenty of exercise. As puppies, they are full of fun, fast learners, and lively. They are ideal for active, sociable families who have the time and energy to train and provide them with useful household tasks or play. They are very affectionate and willing to please.

△ Adult
Adults are lively and suit owners who enjoy exercise and training these energetic dogs.

English Cocker Spaniel

Size *29–33lb (13–15kg), 15–16in (38–41cm)*
Character *Docile, active, affectionate*
Exercise *High*
Grooming *Regular brushing, especially the ears*

English Cocker Spaniels were bred to work as gun dogs and so are lively, responsive, and can be easily trained to retrieve. As puppies, their sweet appearance belies a very strong character. It is wise to set the ground rules and boundaries early with this breed to prevent control problems or disobedience later. They can be possessive of toys and food, and so early training is essential. English Cocker Spaniels have been one of the more popular breeds for many years, due in part to their loving, happy temperament. Their relatively small size makes them an ideal pet for active families. Accustom them to grooming and handling early, paying particular attention to their ears and feathering.

◁ Adult
Ranging in color from golden to black, English Cocker Spaniels need plenty of exercise and play to be contented and well behaved.

Cocker Spaniel

Called the American Cocker Spaniel outside the US, this dog has had a different breed standard from the English one since the late 19th century. Energetic, sensitive, and strong-willed, it has a distinctive high domed head.

Springer Spaniel

Size *49–53lb (22–24kg), 19–20in (48–51cm)*
Character *Energetic, playful, enthusiastic*
Exercise *Very high*
Grooming *Moderate*

Springer Spaniels are friendly and sociable, and it is rare to find one with a bad temperament. Consequently, they make ideal pets for active families with children and are always eager to please. They were bred to flush or "spring" game birds and return them to the handlers once shot. The downside is that their activity levels are higher than many owners can deal with. It is almost impossible to wear them out and they are always looking for things to do. Teach puppies how to retrieve and play games early in life so that exercising them is easier when they are older.

Long, hairy ears need regular maintenance

△ **Adult**
Springer Spaniels can be black and white or liver and white in color. Their silky coats need regular grooming.

Shar Pei

Size *35–44lb (16–20kg), 18–20in (46–51cm)*
Character *Aloof, reserved, loyal*
Exercise *Moderate*
Grooming *Time is needed to care for deep skin folds*

Shar Peis share a common ancestor with the Chow Chow and can be aloof and indifferent. Puppies need good socialization to ensure they become well adjusted. Due to the fashion to exaggerate their skin folds, some have trouble opening their eyes fully and veterinary care may be needed to check they can see properly.

△ **Adult**
Adults are quiet and aloof and can prove to be a disappointing pet for owners who want close companionship.

Bulldog

Size *51–55lb (23–25kg), 12–14in (30–36cm)*
Character *Sociable, courageous, loyal*
Exercise *Minimal*
Grooming *Minimal*

Bulldogs are stoic and affectionate, but suffer from an unnaturally proportioned body, which makes movement and breathing difficult for them. They cannot exercise much without becoming tired, especially in hot weather, and are prone to snoring. Puppies are friendly and sweet-natured, but have a hard bite due to their large skull width.

△ **Adult**
Adults usually have health problems, but triumph over this adversity with an indomitable spirit.

Bull Terrier

Size *53–62lb (24–28kg), 21–22in (53–56cm)*
Character *Feisty, persistent, loyal*
Exercise *Moderate to high*
Grooming *Minimal*

Puppies of this breed are sweet-natured and playful. As adults, they tend to be obsessive and determined, and so it is wise to channel their energy into games with toys from an early age. Bull Terriers suit active families who can give them plenty of stimulation, exercise, and play.

◁ **Adult**
Bulldogs were crossed with English White Terriers in the 19th century to produce the Bull Terrier. They come in a variety of colors.

Large dogs

Large dogs are suitable for people who have plenty of time and space. They can look impressive, but need careful training and many play sessions to use up energy.

Big dogs fit in well with families who have an active lifestyle and lots of energy. They are well suited to families with older children, who can entertain and have fun with them.

With large dogs, everything is bigger, from exercise through to bedding and food bills. Many people enjoy being out with a large dog, and they make impressive pets if they are well trained. Although showing off your large dog can be fun, a lot of time needs to be set aside every day for walks and play, even on days when time is precious, or you need to work, or the weather is bad.

◁ Born to run
Dalmatians need plenty of off-leash exercise to keep them happy, and make good pets for active owners who enjoy long walks.

◁ Bundle of energy
Although easy to exercise when young, large dogs such as Golden Retrievers need plenty of walks and play sessions to keep them contented.

Large dogs can help you feel better protected in your house and there is more to hug when you need a friend. Expenses are larger, from insurance premiums to kennel fees, and more time is needed to clean up after those big muddy paws or shed hair.

Border Collie

Size *31–49lb (14–22kg), 18–21in (46–54cm)*
Character *Intelligent, reactive, close-bonding*
Exercise *Very high*
Grooming *Moderate*

Bred for generations to work all day herding sheep, the Border Collie is fast, loves chasing, and is extremely energetic. Puppies are lively, quick to learn, and playful. Border Collies suit active families who will spend a lot of time socializing, playing, training, and inventing interesting activities to use up their pets' considerable mental and physical energy.

◁ Adult
Border Collies can be sensitive, and may develop noise phobias if they are not properly acclimatized to loud sounds early in life.

△ Working ancestry
Originally bred to herd sheep on the English and Scottish borders, Border Collies are still popular as sheepdogs.

△ Playful puppy
Owners need to channel energies into play with toys and train their puppy regularly from an early age to ensure good control later.

Siberian Husky

Size *35–61lb (16–27.5kg), 20–24in (51–60cm)*
Character *Active, intelligent, independent*
Exercise *Very high*
Grooming *Extensive daily grooming*

Siberian Huskies are predatory, independent hunters with the ability to run all day. They make affectionate pets who have a real love for the family, but they can be difficult to control outside. Puppies are cute and inquisitive. Training needs to be done early—after puberty, they will not work hard to please you.

△ **Adult**
Bred to run distances hauling sleds, Huskies are energetic, strong, and sociable within their family.

Basset Hound

Size *40–60lb (18–27kg), 13–15in (33–38cm)*
Character *Sweet-natured, sociable, independent*
Exercise *High*
Grooming *Minimal*

Basset Hounds are large dogs with a poorly designed body that has been exaggerated by breeders, creating short limbs, a long back, excess skin, and long ears. They have a happy, easygoing, hound temperament and puppies are sweet-natured, yet they can be hard to control on a walk and are difficult to recall once on a scent.

△ **Adult**
Basset Hounds were bred for hunting rabbits by following their scent.

Bearded Collie

Size *40–66lb (18–30kg), 20–22in (50–56cm)*
Character *Playful, active, sensitive*
Exercise *Very high*
Grooming *Extensive daily grooming*

Bearded Collies are sensitive and close-bonding, with a strong desire to chase. They suit gentle, considerate families who will socialize them well and channel their urge to chase into games with toys. As puppies, they are playful and learn quickly. Gradually accustom them to being brushed and combed early in life so that daily coat care is easier.

◁ **Adult**
Adults have a thick, full coat of long, silky hair that needs daily grooming to keep it in good condition.

Australian Shepherd

Size *35–70lb (16–32kg), 18–23in (46–58cm)*
Character *Intelligent, strong-willed, active*
Exercise *Very high*
Grooming *Moderate*

Almost unknown in Australia, this breed was developed on ranches in the western US for herding sheep. Puppies are playful and need plenty of socialization. When mature, they have an intense work ethic and a tough character, and suit strong-willed owners who will channel this into useful work or plentiful play.

◁ **Adult**
Adults are loyal, devoted, and energetic, and thrive in families where they can be given lots to do.

Rough Collie

Size *40–66lb (18–30kg), 20–24in (50–60cm)*
Character *Sensitive, loyal, gentle*
Exercise *Moderate*
Grooming *Extensive daily grooming*

Once bred to herd sheep, Rough Collies are intelligent and close-bonding. As puppies, they are sensitive and shy, so need careful socialization. Introduce them gradually to all the things they will encounter in later life so that they develop into relaxed adults. Rough Collies love playing chase games.

△ **Adult**
Sensitive and responsive, adults make good pets for gentle families who will take special care to keep them socialized.

Standard Poodle

Size *45–70lb (20.5–32kg), over 15in (38cm)*
Character *Intelligent, good-natured, active*
Exercise *High to very high*
Grooming *Daily grooming and regular clipping*

△ **Adult**
Adults are lively and intelligent, but also careful and deliberate; they make good pets for interactive owners.

Standard Poodles are intelligent and graceful. The pom-poms seen on show dogs are exaggerations of fur left to protect the joints of working dogs, but most pet owners opt for a clip that is one length all over, which is more practical for everyday life. As puppies, Standard Poodles are lively, affectionate, and playful. They enjoy working and are quick to learn lessons. Daily coat care is essential and puppies need to get used to being groomed from an early age.

Airedale Terrier

Size *20–22.5kg (44–50lb), 22–24in (56–61cm)*
Character *Intelligent, courageous, loyal*
Exercise *Moderate*
Grooming *Requires periodic stripping of dead coat*

The Airedale Terrier is the largest of the terriers and was once bred to hunt otters and badgers, and to act as a guard dog. Airedale Terriers are usually good with children. They can be protective, so puppies need careful socialization to ensure they grow up to be friendly adults. Owners therefore need to be determined and experienced.

◁ **Adult**
Airedales are loyal and protective toward their family and make robust playmates for children if well socialized.

Dalmatian

Size *50–55lb (22.5–25kg), 20–24in (50–61cm)*
Character *Independent, outgoing, sociable*
Exercise *Very high*
Grooming *Minimal*

First bred to run alongside carriages of the wealthy, Dalmatians are natural runners. Owners need to teach puppies a good recall so they can get them back when older. This breed suits active people who are happy to walk or run for long distances. Dalmatians can be independent-minded, so good socialization and training are needed when young.

△ **Adult**
Although adults are distinguished by their spots, these do not appear until puppies are around 2 weeks old.

Short and spotted coat

German Shorthaired Pointer

Size *44–66lb (20–30kg), 24–26in (60–65cm)*
Character *Sociable, energetic, playful*
Exercise *Very high*
Grooming *Minimal*

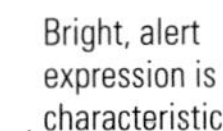

German Shorthaired Pointers were bred in the 19th century to be general-purpose gun dogs. They are energetic and willing to please. Owners need to be active, with plenty of time to devote to keeping these dogs busy. Puppies are inquisitive and playful and need lots of games and activities to keep them occupied. Teach them to retrieve well from an early age to make exercising easier in later life. As adults, German Shorthaired Pointers are enthusiastic and loving, always ready for action, and with tremendous energy that can become a problem unless it is channeled into daily walks, training, and play. Their thin, smooth coat makes for easy grooming, although they can shed small hairs that weave their way into fabric.

Bright, alert expression is characteristic

△ **Adult**
The undercoat of an adult German Shorthaired Pointer is protected by guard hairs, which provide water resistance and warmth.

Excellent gun dog

Known to be versatile and easy to train, the German Shorthaired Pointer makes an excellent working dog. Bred to hunt, point, and retrieve, they are good all-rounders, compared with other dogs that are more specialized, such as the Setters.

Boxer

Size *55–70lb (25–32kg), 21–25in (53–63cm)*
Character *Exuberant, playful, friendly*
Exercise *Very high*
Grooming *Minimal*

Boxers are boisterous and exuberant. They need plenty of socialization when young and suit active, lively families who will keep them entertained. They are very loving to owners and can be a good playmate for children if trained well from an early age. Their flattened faces can make them prone to dribbling and snoring.

◁ **Adult**
Boxers live up to their name with their tendency to "box" with their front paws during play.

Labrador Retriever

Size *55–79lb (25–36kg), 22–24in (55–62cm)*
Character *Docile, sociable, playful*
Exercise *Very high*
Grooming *Minimal*

Labradors have been a long-standing favorite of families for good reason. They are good-natured and easygoing. When well trained and socialized, they can be friendly to all, but still retain enough awareness to bark at anything suspicious. Bred for and still used as gun dogs, they are energetic, willing to please, and ready to join in or help out at a moment's notice. As a result, they have been widely used as assistance dogs, including guide dogs and hearing dogs, and for drug and other scent detection duties. As pets, they are happy to be helpful around the house if trained to do useful tasks. They love food and have impressive appetites, so it is important to monitor their weight carefully. Owners will need to be careful not to allow puppies to raid tabletops and pantries when young, so that no bad habits develop. It is also sensible to develop a good retrieve early in life to make exercise and recalls easier later on. Puppies are playful and energetic, and it is easy to channel their natural exuberance into games with toys.

Bright, intelligent eyes

Long, well-proportioned tail

△ **Adult**
High-spirited Labradors love getting wet and are fast swimmers. Take time to accustom puppies to water.

△ **Exuberant**
Labradors have a fun-loving nature and really enjoy playing with toys, which makes them a good pet for families.

Willing workers

Labradors are used for many different types of work. Some are trained to help the disabled with everyday tasks, such as shopping. Their willingness to please and their high drive allows them to work hard all day long for minimal reward, while their kind temperament makes them good companions.

△ **High energy**
Working strains are still used for gun dog work—these dogs have plenty of energy and the stamina to keep going all day.

Fit for life
Young Labradors need lots of exercise to stay healthy. Be careful not to overfeed them since they are prone to putting on weight, especially after being neutered.

Hovawart

Size *55–90lb (25–41kg), 23–28in (58–70cm)*
Character *Intelligent, loyal, protective*
Exercise *Very high*
Grooming *Moderate*

Clever, energetic, and protective, Hovawarts can be imposing when defending their family and territory. Careful socialization and training is needed to ensure they are tolerant of strangers. Puppies of this breed are active, loving, and quick to learn. They benefit from owners who can channel their energies into games.

Flat, long, wavy fur

△ **Adult**
Hovawarts are loyal and make good watchdogs. The name means "guardian of property" in German.

Belgian Shepherd

Size *61–63lb (27.5–28.5kg), 22–26in (56–66cm)*
Character *Reactive, intelligent, protective*
Exercise *Very high*
Grooming *Depends on variety*

There are four breeds of Belgian Shepherd—the Malinois, the Tervueren, the Groenendael, and the Laekenois—but all have similar temperaments. As adults, they are sensitive and reactive, and like to chase. Puppies need careful socialization to ensure they grow up to be well-adjusted, and their high energy levels need to be channeled into toy play from an early age.

△ **Adult**
Belgian Shepherds thrive with easygoing owners who are good leaders.

Golden Retriever

Size *60–79lb (27–36kg), 20–24in (51–61cm)*
Character *Sociable, playful, kind*
Exercise *High*
Grooming *Daily*

The Golden Retriever has been high on the most popular dogs list for many years for good reason. This active dog, originally bred and still used as a gun dog, is affectionate, easygoing, and calm. As puppies, they have boundless energy and extroverted natures. They are eager to please and learn fast, making training easy. Some strains can be possessive, so it is important to teach puppies early in life not to be worried about hands coming near their toys or food. Golden Retrievers suit fun, active families where there is plenty of stimulation, and daily exercise and play.

△ **Good playmate**
Ideal for families with children, Golden Retrievers love to play. Be careful that your dog does not become possessive over toys.

Long, thick, wavy coat

▷ **Adult**
Golden Retrievers should be groomed daily, because their thick coats shed lots of hair.

German Wirehaired Pointer

Size *60–70lb (27–32kg), 24–27in (61–68cm)*
Character *Docile, energetic, playful*
Exercise *Very high*
Grooming *Minimal*

Like their short-haired cousins, German Wirehaired Pointers were developed as general-purpose, rugged gun dogs. Consequently, they have lots of energy. They can be a little sensitive and wary of strangers, so need careful socialization as puppies. Willing to please and ready for action, dogs of this breed need gentle but firm handling to get the best out of them. These affectionate dogs do best with owners who can devote plenty of time to walks and activities.

◁ **Adult**
Adults have a wiry coat to provide added protection for gun dog work. They develop a short beard with their adult coat.

Beard hair will need regular cleaning

Flat-coated Retriever

Size *55–79lb (25–36kg), 22–24in (56–61cm)*
Character *Gentle, affectionate, outgoing*
Exercise *High*
Grooming *Minimal*

Flat-coated Retrievers have a tolerant and attentive nature, and make ideal pets for families. They are always ready and eager to retrieve and, as puppies, are extremely playful. Although rarely clumsy or boisterous, they do need plenty to do and regular walks to use up their surplus energy and to allow them to relax in the house. Flat-coated Retrievers do not make good watchdogs or guard dogs since they are happy to welcome anyone. This makes them ideal for novice or sociable owners. They can be a little on the slow side when it comes to learning, so patience is needed during training.

△ **Family friend**
These sociable, easygoing dogs make friends effortlessly, and really enjoy being part of a family.

▷ **Adult**
Flat-coated Retrievers were originally bred in England in the 19th century to be versatile gun dogs.

German Shepherd Dog

Size *62–97lb (28–44kg), 22–26in (55–66cm)*
Character *Intelligent, protective, loyal*
Exercise *Very high*
Grooming *Daily, especially for long-coated varieties*

Puppies of this breed are sensitive, quick to learn, responsive, and playful. They can be shy and need careful socialization to help them to become well-adjusted adults, able to take anything in their stride. Socialization must begin early, so be sure to find a breeder who will spend the time and effort needed to prepare the puppies well for everyday life as a pet. Adults are intelligent, loyal, and close-bonding. German Shepherds are often called "one person" dogs, but they will readily bond with all those they trust. They are very easy to train if a kind, positive approach is taken, and they make excellent working dogs. They are also good watchdogs and defenders of the home. Careful training is needed to keep this protective tendency from spreading to visitors and delivery people, and barking needs to be controlled so that it does not become excessive. German Shepherds are energetic and make good pets for active owners. They love to play and their drive to chase should be channeled into games with toys from an early age.

◁ **Adult**
Modern breeders have curved the back, leading to compromised hips and legs that weaken with age. Take time to find a healthy, straight-backed puppy.

Rhodesian Ridgeback

Size *65–85lb (29.5–38.5kg), 24–27in (60–69cm)*
Character *Independent, discerning, protective*
Exercise *High*
Grooming *Minimal*

Rhodesian Ridgebacks are loving and loyal to their families and good with children. They need plenty of socialization with strangers and other dogs when young. Their love of chasing, particularly other animals and fast-moving vehicles, can lead to control problems on walks, so recall training is essential. Puppies are more eager to please than adults, so train them early.

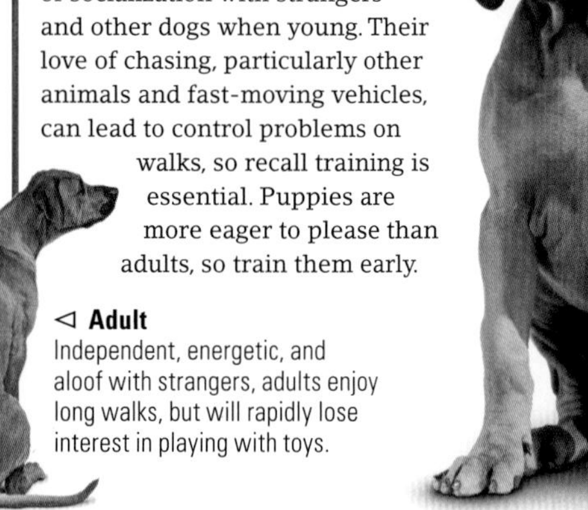

◁ **Adult**
Independent, energetic, and aloof with strangers, adults enjoy long walks, but will rapidly lose interest in playing with toys.

Doberman Pinscher

Size *66–88lb (30–40kg), 24–28in (60–70cm)*
Character *Intelligent, alert, protective*
Exercise *High*
Grooming *Minimal*

The Doberman Pinscher was bred in the 19th century to be a guard dog, but many of today's dogs have lost a lot of the sharpness they once had and make good pets. They are highly intelligent and easily trained, provided they have experienced, strong-willed owners who have plenty of time to help use up their considerable energy.

△ **Adult**
Adults can look imposing but worry easily. They do best with gentle yet determined owners.

Giant Schnauzer

Size *70–77lb (32–35kg), 24–28in (60–70cm)*
Character *Intelligent, loyal, protective*
Exercise *High*
Grooming *Daily grooming and regular stripping/clipping*

These large dogs are good-natured, intelligent, and protective, and require experienced owners. Bred for cattle droving and guarding, they can look imposing and need careful socialization and training when young. As puppies, Giant Schnauzers are playful and it is easy to channel their energies into games with toys.

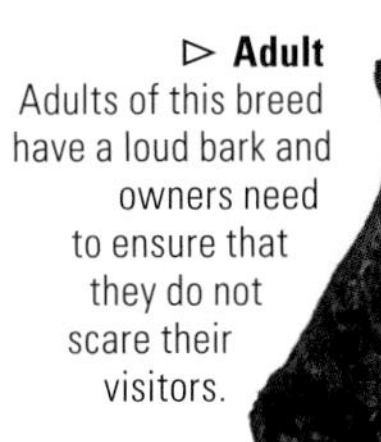

▷ **Adult**
Adults of this breed have a loud bark and owners need to ensure that they do not scare their visitors.

Weimaraner

Size *70–86lb (32–39kg), 22–27in (56–69cm)*
Character *Energetic, exuberant, playful*
Exercise *Very high*
Grooming *Minimal*

Developed as general-purpose gun dogs, Weimaraners are energetic and need lots of exercise to be calm. Without sufficient exercise, they can become boisterous and exuberant, so before purchasing a puppy, it is vital to consider if you have enough energy to keep up with them, particularly when they are young. They are physically sensitive and can feel the cold unless kept active. As puppies, they are lively and eager to please. Channel their energies into retrieve games with toys for easy exercising in later life.

◁ **Adult**
Loyal and intelligent, the Weimaraner is elegant and exuberant, with enough energy to keep on the go all day.

Akita

Size *77–110lb (35–50kg), 24–28in (60–70cm)*
Character *Aloof, protective, independent*
Exercise *High*
Grooming *Extensive daily grooming*

Akitas are aloof, independent, and dignified. Bred to show little emotion, they suit experienced owners who want an independent, imposing-looking dog. Careful socialization is necessary, especially with other dogs, if they are to be good with them in later life. They are clean, quiet, and calm, and make a loving, loyal guard dog for families.

△ **Adult**
Akitas were originally bred for bear hunting and dog fighting in the 17th century.

Dogue de Bordeaux

Size *79–99lb (36–45kg), 23–27in (58–69cm)*
Character *Courageous, loyal, protective*
Exercise *High*
Grooming *Minimal*

Determined owners are needed to control these powerful, strong-willed dogs. Dogue de Bordeaux puppies are playful and fun-loving, but they require lots of training and early socialization, particularly with other dogs, to be well behaved in later life. The shape of the jaw causes this breed to snore and dribble profusely.

△ **Adult**
The energetic Dogue de Bordeaux is thought to have originated in France as a pit-fighting dog.

Extra-large dogs

Extra-large dogs are for enthusiasts who have plenty of space and time to devote to care and maintenance. They are often gentle giants, but unfortunately they tend to have shorter lifespans than smaller dogs.

Extra-large dogs make an impressive statement and can make owners feel safer, but they also bring a bigger price tag for maintenance. They are not as portable as smaller dogs and often necessitate the purchase of an extra-large car for transportation. Surprisingly, extra-large dogs rarely need as much exercise as their lighter-weight, more agile cousins, and so are more suitable for owners who like to live life at a slower pace. They will, however, require a large backyard where they can speed up and slow down in good time without having to turn sharply, especially when they are puppies and have less control over their large frames. Potential owners should also consider the consequences of owning a dog they cannot lift or carry if it gets into difficulties, or that they cannot hold back if it is really determined to get somewhere.

▷ **Powerhouse**
With size comes strength, and Bullmastiff owners need to be physically strong to control these giants of the dog world.

Leonberger

Size *75–110lb (34–50kg), 26–31in (65–80cm)*
Character *Calm, protective, affectionate*
Exercise *High*
Grooming *Daily*

The Leonberger was developed in the 19th century by mixing Newfoundlands and Saint Bernards with a few other breeds. The result is a gentle and affectionate dog, which has become popular as a family guardian and companion. Leonbergers are good and careful with children but can be protective—good training and early socialization will ensure that this does not lead to problems. Make sure that you teach them to walk nicely on a loose leash at a young age, to enable safe outings and easy walks in later life. Their heavy coats need a lot of maintenance, so Leonbergers should be groomed daily.

◁ **Adult**
Adults often overheat in normal temperatures, leading to excessive panting and drooling.

True crossbreed

The Mayor of Leonberg, Germany, set out to breed a dog that resembled the lion on the town crest. He crossed Newfoundlands with the ancestors of the Saint Bernard, together with several other breeds, and the result was the Leonberger. The breed was refined later to create the black mask and darker coat.

Bernese Mountain Dog

Size *88–97lb (40–44kg), 23–28in (58–70cm)*
Character *Calm, protective, sociable*
Exercise *Moderate*
Grooming *Daily*

Affectionate and loving to their owners, Bernese Mountain Dogs can make good family dogs. They are naturally protective, so careful socialization is needed during puppyhood to prevent this from becoming a problem. Their ancestors were bred to guard, drive cattle, and pull carts, but this strength can be managed by early training, especially how to walk nicely on a loose leash.

△ Adult
Uninhibited by their large frames, adults are energetic and need strong owners when taken for walks.

Rottweiler

Size *90–110lb (41–50kg), 23–27in (58–69cm)*
Character *Protective, loyal, alert*
Exercise *High*
Grooming *Minimal*

Rottweiler puppies are playful and fun-loving. They are also intelligent and quick to figure things out, so it is important to help them learn only good habits. As adults, they are imposing and strong, so careful socialization is needed to avoid overprotective behavior from developing later in life. Rottweilers are best suited to determined, experienced owners who will train them to behave well and provide an outlet for their energy by giving them plenty to keep them occupied.

△ Adult
Originally bred in Germany to drive cattle and for protection, Rottweilers are strong and confident.

Powerful hind limbs

Bullmastiff

Size *90–130lb (41–59kg), 25–27in (64–69cm)*
Character *Courageous, protective, loyal*
Exercise *Moderate*
Grooming *Minimal*

△ Adult
Usually friendly and docile, Bullmastiffs can be vigorous in defense of their family and need careful handling.

Once used by gamekeepers to catch poachers, these dogs have a powerful body and a protective nature. They need plenty of socialization and early training to ensure safety for all in later life. Bullmastiffs suit experienced, determined owners. Puppies are playful, good-natured, and tolerant with children and other animals.

Loose, wrinkly skin allows for fast growth

Strong limbs support their weight

Newfoundland

Size *110–150lb (50–68kg), 26–28in (66–71cm)*
Character *Calm, sociable, affectionate*
Exercise *Moderate*
Grooming *Daily*

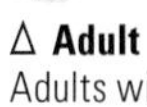

△ Adult
Adults will spend a lot of time panting, drooling, and trying to keep cool.

Bred to help fishermen in Canada, the Newfoundland is a gentle, easygoing dog with a sociable temperament and a love of water. Puppies are fun-loving, but can be slow to learn. Their thick coat can make them too hot in normal temperatures, leading to excessive panting and drooling. They will be strong when mature, and so from an early age they need to learn to walk on a loose leash without pulling.

Flat, dense, and oily coat

Great Dane

Size *110–176lb (50–80kg), 31–36in (79–92cm)*
Character *Playful, independent, affectionate*
Exercise *Moderate*
Grooming *Minimal*

These gentle giants were originally bred to hunt wild boar. Today's Great Danes have retained the instincts and desire to chase other animals and can run fast, especially when young. This can lead to control problems on walks. Great Danes have a true hound temperament and are sociable and affectionate to those they know, but also independent, with a mind of their own. With good socialization, puppies can grow up to become well-balanced, friendly adults. Due to their tendency to chase things that run, train Great Danes early to come back when called and to retrieve toys instead.

Harlequin coat

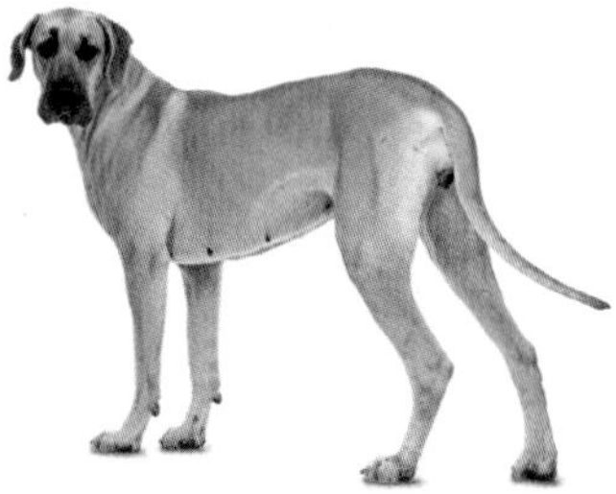

Fawn coat

△ Adult
Among the world's tallest dogs, Great Danes have a range of coat colors, including blue, brindle, and black, as well as fawn and harlequin.

Strong limbs to support a large body

Big feet give an indication of future size

Saint Bernard

Size *110–201lb (50–91kg), 24–28in (61–71cm)*
Character *Gentle, sociable, loyal*
Exercise *Moderate*
Grooming *Daily*

Saint Bernards are gentle giants and, as puppies, they are affectionate and fun-loving. Plenty of training early in life is advisable so that you can control them when they have grown large and strong. Bred to rescue those stuck in snow, Saint Bernards are often too hot in temperate climates, so panting and drooling can be a messy problem as they try to stay cool under their thick coats.

△ Adult
Easygoing and usually friendly, Saint Bernards are happy to please owners and can make good pets for families.

Big, loose lips can be prone to dribbling

Mongrels and **crossbreeds**

Cross-bred and mongrel puppies can make lovely pets. Each one is unique in appearance and character, although when you take one home, you are never quite sure what it will grow into.

Mongrels are a mixture of many breeds, while crossbreeds have dogs of two breeds as parents. Mongrels are rare in countries where stray dogs are regularly picked up by local authorities.

Crossbreeds are often created by breeders who want the best of all the characteristics found in two breeds. This also widens the gene pool and reduces the risk of genetic disease. Recently, there has been an increase in the number of people buying crossbreeds—this may be due to owners trying to avoid the many inherited conditions present in pedigree (pure-bred) dogs.

◁ The Sprocker
The product of two spaniels, a Springer and a Cocker, the Sprocker's lively and hard-working character is inherited from both parents.

◁ An enigma
This German Shepherd Dog-mix puppy's future temperament and size will remain a mystery until he is older.

It is not always easy to predict how puppies with a mix of genes will turn out, or how large they will grow. But if you are happy to take a chance, you will own a dog that is unlike all others.

Inherited good looks
Most mixed-breed puppies resemble both parents, although some (below and bottom left) closely resemble just one. As with appearance, there will also be a mixture of characteristics.

2

Your new puppy

First steps

Bringing home a puppy after all the preparation and waiting is **exhilarating for any new owner**. Excitement is only natural, especially if there are children in your family. **First impressions** really do count, so make sure you **do a good job of welcoming your puppy into your home**. It will be a **big step** for your puppy to leave his first home, his mother, and his littermates. This section explains how to make all the necessary **preparations before your puppy arrives**. It will also help you to **figure out what he needs in these first few weeks** without his mother, so he can **settle into his new home** and new life **as quickly as possible**.

FAMILY LIFE
It will take a few weeks for your puppy to settle in, get used to his surroundings, and learn to live successfully with a new family.

Bringing your **puppy home**

Your puppy's first day at his new home will be fun for you, but can be unsettling for him. Knowing what to do, while at the breeder's and when he gets home, will help your puppy adjust to his new life.

When to collect

A week in a young puppy's life makes a big difference (p.63), so you should aim to take your puppy home by the time he is 8 weeks old. At this age, he will be weaned, he will have learned some play skills with his littermates, and he will have been taught some lessons by his mother. At the same time, he will still be young enough to learn to live easily with a human family. Don't be tempted to leave your puppy with the breeder until he is 9 or 10 weeks old. Those extra weeks may cause him to become very dog-focused, rather than human-focused, and therefore be a less successful pet than if he were taken home earlier and taught to live with humans.

Making preparations

Before your puppy arrives, have a good look around your home and backyard from a puppy's eye level and pick up anything that your puppy may chew that could hurt him. Check for potentially poisonous plants or berries in the yard and remove or block access to them. Close any puppy-sized holes in fences and make sure that your puppy cannot get underneath or through a barrier to somewhere he might be harmed.

Think also about where your puppy should sleep. It needs to be somewhere warm and in the central part of the house, where he will have some company, but it also needs to be quiet, so he can rest easily and not be distracted by household activity. It is not necessary to buy an expensive bed for him until he is older and past the chewing stages. A strong cardboard box will do if you cut an entrance into it and line it with an old, thick blanket. Alternatively, you could invest in a strong plastic bed of a size that will fit your puppy when he is older, and put a thick pad of bedding inside it for him to sleep on.

"You should **aim to take** your **puppy home** by the time he is **8 weeks old.**"

◁ **Heading home** Bring home your puppy at 8 weeks, rather than at 9 or 10 weeks; extra weeks in the litter will make him more interested in other dogs than you in later life.

▷ **Using a stair gate** A stair gate can help keep your puppy in one room when necessary, but still allow him to watch what you are doing and not feel too alone.

▷ **Useful separations**
To give your puppy somewhere to rest without being disturbed, the playpen should be a no-go zone for children. It can also be used to allow children to have some uninterrupted playtime.

▽ **Settling down**
Use food and chew toys to encourage your puppy to go into the playpen and relax. Always make sure he is well exercised and has gone to the bathroom before shutting him inside.

The playpen

It is a good idea to purchase a playpen for your puppy. This is much better than a metal crate, since there is room for a bed and also newspaper, so that your puppy can go to the bathroom if he needs to. The playpen can be left open when your puppy is in the house, so that he has the option of going back to bed if he wants to. The playpen can also be used for times when you are too busy to concentrate on him, or when you need to go out. This will prevent your puppy from learning bad habits when you are not there to supervise him. Don't reward any barking or jumping up with attention, and don't leave him there for longer than 1 hour before taking him outside to go to the bathroom and for a play session.

◁ **New addition**
Allow plenty of time for your puppy to settle into your home. You may spend much of those first days just watching him and giving him attention.

Preparing for your puppy

- Get a week's supply of puppy food from the breeder.
- Take a piece of bedding from the nest as a comforter for your puppy on his first nights (pp.58–9).
- Ask the breeder for a feeding/housebreaking chart.
- Obtain a pedigree registration certificate from the Kennel Club.
- You will need a chart showing your puppy's breeding line, and a vaccination certificate (if applicable).

Introducing the **family**

The secret to easy introductions is to keep calm and prevent bad experiences. This requires careful planning and supervision. Good introductions will help ensure successful future relationships.

First impressions

When you arrive home with your puppy, take him into the yard so he can explore and relieve himself. He may be overwhelmed by the journey and feeling a little sick, so give him time to move around and relax until he feels better.

Once your puppy has recovered from the journey and feels more confident, it is time to introduce him to any other canine residents in your house. This is best done in the backyard if your existing dog is good with puppies. If you are unsure about how your older dog will react, introduce them in a big, open space away from home territory where other dogs don't go (since your puppy won't yet be vaccinated). Give them plenty of space to escape from each other if they need to, and try not to crowd them or intervene unless one of them is getting scared or turning aggressive. If necessary, hold back the more exuberant one and give the other time to relax before trying again. Not all adult dogs will accept a puppy's advances, so watch out for signs of distress that may result in aggression from your existing dog. If you see any such signs, distract your puppy or hold him for a while to give your other dog a break. When they have gotten to know each other in the yard, allow them into the house—but first pick up anything that could be fought over, such as chew toys or beds. To prevent jealousy, it may be best to ignore the puppy briefly and make a fuss of your older dog until things calm down.

◁ **Good introductions**
Humans are less overwhelming if they are sitting down and offering treats, so this is a good way for other family members to greet their new puppy.

▽ **Meeting children**
Let your puppy approach the children for games with a toy or food, but supervise carefully so that he cannot jump on them or frighten them.

◁ **Early exploration**
Allow time for your puppy to explore the yard, relax, sniff scents, and go to the bathroom before entering your house for the first time.

△ **New friends**
Not all adult dogs will tolerate a puppy's advances, so watch carefully for signs of distress that may result in aggressive behavior from your existing dog.

Any children in the family will naturally be excited about the new addition to the household. Run through the procedure of introductions with the children beforehand, explaining that the puppy will feel more comfortable about meeting them if they are seated and offering small, tasty treats on the flat of their hands. If you have another dog, it may be advisable to put him in another room while the puppy meets the children. Ask them to let the puppy come to them, rather than allowing them to crowd around to pet him, which might be overwhelming for him. Children also need to know not to pick the puppy up, since this may be uncomfortable and unsettling for him.

It is better to let your puppy settle in properly before you introduce him to other pets, such as cats and rabbits. Always restrain the puppy, so that he knows that chasing is not acceptable. Keep calm and wait until the other pet has moved away before releasing your puppy.

△ **Meeting the cat**
Cats can be scared by an enthusiastic puppy, so restrain your puppy carefully to reduce his movements and prevent him from approaching.

Happy households

Successful relationships are built on successful encounters, so make sure an adult is always present to supervise interactions involving your puppy. If someone is always on hand to ensure both parties have fun and are never upset or overwhelmed, good relationships should rapidly develop between the puppy and all others living in your household—human and animal.

"Not all **adult dogs** will tolerate a **puppy's advances,** so **you** will **need to be careful."**

Alone at home

Dogs are a social species and can become distressed when left alone, especially when they are puppies. We need to teach them slowly and carefully to accept being by themselves.

Separation

In nature, young puppies stay with their mother and littermates until adolescence, then start to move away from the nest area to explore, becoming more independent as they do so. When we take puppies away from their litter at 8 weeks, they are still young and vulnerable, and they will try to find someone in the household to bond with. If separated from company, they quickly become distressed. This is their natural response, and forcing them to endure isolation at this time will make them very fearful of being left alone later.

What to do at night

Leaving a puppy alone on his first night in a new house will distress him. To avoid this, put your puppy in your bedroom, in a high-sided box, so that he can be reassured by your presence. Once he has learned to be alone for 30 minutes during the day, his nighttime box can be gradually moved out of the bedroom and, eventually, be placed in the room you want him to sleep in.

Many adult dogs will bark, howl, become destructive, or urinate in the house when left alone. These behaviors stem from being left alone for too long as young puppies. To avoid such separation anxiety developing, teaching a young puppy to accept isolation gradually is very important.

Isolation tolerance

Once your puppy has settled into your home, wait until he is tired and ready to sleep. Take him out to go to the bathroom and then play a short game with him to use up any excess energy. Take him back into the house and use a treat to encourage him to go into his playpen and get on his bed. Close the pen and leave him to rest. Ignore small barks, but return if he becomes very distressed. If you do return, don't talk to him, just stay in the room until he calms down. Leave him alone again as he settles, and, once asleep, open the door, so he can come find you when he wakes up.

Gradually build up his tolerance to being left alone. Go slowly, but leave him in his pen several times a day, so that by the end of the first week, he is spending quite a lot of time by himself. You can then start to leave him alone for short periods in different rooms of the house and, eventually, in other places such as the car. When starting for the first time in a new place, always begin by leaving your puppy for just a minute or two before returning, and then slowly increase the amount of time he is left alone.

△ **See you later**
Stair gates allow your puppy to get used to isolation while you are in sight and, later, with the door closed.

▷ **Back soon**
Only leave your puppy alone in the car for short periods to start with, so that he can gradually get used to the experience.

Bonding session
Puppies enjoy being close to those who look after them. They will work hard to be with you, which makes being alone so much harder for them to cope with.

Getting to know your puppy

Although it is natural for us to treat puppies like children, they are a **different species**, with different **motivations and needs**. If we are to form **successful relationships** with our dogs, we need to find out about these differences, and **learn how dogs communicate** with us and with each other. Understanding **how dogs see the world** will help us to treat them more appropriately, and have **realistic expectations** of them. By following the advice in this section, you will end up with a contented puppy, who will find it easier to learn to **enjoy life** in the **strange world of humans**.

BRUSH UP
Finding out about how your puppy thinks and why he behaves in certain ways will help you to understand him better.

Understanding your puppy

Puppies are unlike adult dogs in many ways, and they also sense the world in a different way than humans do. Knowing what these differences are helps us treat puppies more appropriately.

Young brains

Puppies have shorter attention spans than adult dogs, and so it is important to keep their training sessions short. If each session is about 3 minutes long, they have sufficient time to learn without becoming too tired. Young puppies are more easily distracted than older dogs, so it is advisable to teach them in a quiet place where they can concentrate until they become more mature. Their developing brains also need more rest—make sure you allow plenty of time each day for your puppy to sleep and recover from active play, training, and socialization.

Another difference between puppies and adult dogs is that puppies are dependent on those around them for care, whereas adults are much more independent. This works in our favor—until puberty begins at around 6 months of age, puppies will work very hard to please us. Teaching lessons early and using positive techniques is much easier as a result, and puppy owners should make every effort to take advantage of this receptive time. Puppies are also very playful, and play can be used in training so that they learn what we require.

For all the advantages that puppyhood offers, remember that your puppy's young brain is still developing, which means that he will not yet be capable of sophisticated learning, or able to commit much to memory. Because of this, training sessions should be

◁ **Hard work**
Learning is difficult for puppies, and consumes a lot of mental energy as new brain connections are made in the struggle to understand what their owners want from them.

△ **Restorative sleep**
Puppies need plenty of time to rest and sleep after strenuous activities—both mental and physical—enabling them to recuperate and be ready for the next event.

relatively simple, and you will need patience and perseverance to help your puppy learn what you are trying to teach him.

Sensory differences

Puppies see the world in a very different way than humans, and it is useful to consider this when interacting with them. They are very small in relation to us and their surroundings, which gives them a different perspective on the world and on those who are trying to communicate with them. Getting down to their level can help you see things from their point of view.

In addition, our primary sense is our sight, and we use vision to see what is going on in our world. Although dogs can see movement better and have better vision in low-light levels than humans, they see form and detail less clearly. They do not see red or green colors, seeing instead only yellows and blues. A dog's primary sense is its sense of smell. Dogs smell scents in a way that we can only imagine, detecting many more odors than us and at much lower concentrations. This enables them to gather a great deal of information in one sniff, and as a result reduces the importance of eyesight as a sense. Their ears are also more sensitive than ours, enabling them to hear more high-pitched sounds as well as sounds that are farther away.

△ Fast development
A week in a puppy's life is equivalent to about 4 months in a child's life, so make sure you work with your puppy every day.

Age comparisons

Puppies develop much faster than children, so the first year is critical.

PUPPY	HUMAN
0–3 weeks: eyes, ears open	0–1 year
6 weeks: playful, more coordinated	2 years
8 weeks: ready to go to new home	3 years
12 weeks	4 years
16 weeks	6 years
24 weeks: puberty	8 years
8 months	14 years
12 months: beginning of adulthood	20 years
18 months: social maturity	24 years
7 years: middle age	50 years
10 years: onset of old age	70 years
15 years	90 years

△ What humans see
Humans with good eyesight see forms clearly, with pin-sharp detail and in full color. Sight is the primary sense used by humans to gather information about the world around them.

△ What dogs see
Dogs see a world without red or green colors, and in less detail than humans do, but they have a much more acute sense of movement. Their impressive sense of smell is more important to them than sight.

Brand new world
Young puppies like to investigate anything new. They will make decisions about whether objects are safe, fun to play with, or edible, and store the information in their minds for future encounters.

Body language

Dogs communicate with each other and with humans by using body movements and postures. Learning what puppies are saying and how to communicate with them by giving clear signals will help you "talk dog."

Poor verbal skills

Humans have good verbal abilities and the area of the human brain that deals with communication is large. In contrast, dogs have extremely limited verbal skills, because only a small part of their brain is responsible for processing this information. As a result, dogs find it very difficult to learn individual words, and impossible to learn language.

Instead, dogs have evolved to pay particular attention to the body

▽ **Not sure**
The Collie puppy on the right is unsure—he has drawn himself up with raised head and tail to make himself look more imposing and to prevent the other dog from jumping on him.

△ **"Steady up!"**
The Cairn Terrier puppy on the left is a little overwhelmed by the other puppy's boisterous play. He shows concern by sitting down, with his tail tucked under and his ears pinned back.

△ **"Please play!"**
After an active game, the black Spaniel puppy tries to encourage his Collie friend—who is temporarily distracted—to resume play by pawing at him to stimulate a response.

postures and movements of others. They are very attentive to how other dogs posture and display, and our pet dogs watch us in a similar way to find out how we are feeling, and to guess our intentions and next moves.

Learn to interpret

If you watch dogs as they meet in a park, you will be able to see these signals and movements clearly. Do they hold their tails high as a sign of confidence, or do they lower them to show that they are a bit worried about the encounter and may prefer not to get involved? A wagging tail is a way of showing excitement rather than happiness. A stiff tail shows concern, while a relaxed tail indicates a relaxed mind. What position are their ears held in? Ears held back indicate that a dog is worried, while ears held forward signal attention. Watching dogs meeting and playing will help you learn their signals and anticipate what they might do next. The more experience you have of watching dogs, the better you will be able to "read" them. If you are a new owner, try to spend as much time as you can watching dogs interact with other dogs and their owners. This will help you to read your own puppy better, and communicating with him will be easier. In addition, if you learn to recognize when he is feeling worried or upset, you can help him avoid such situations, so that he never has to resort to aggression to solve his problems.

△ **Alarming stare**
This shy puppy turns his head away from the owner's direct stare, exposed teeth, and full attention to avoid an encounter that from his perspective looks a little dangerous.

◁ **This way**
Making your signals clear and consistent will help your puppy to learn what you want him to do much more quickly than if you teach him with words alone (pp.142–3).

> "Our **pet dogs** watch us **carefully** to find out about our **feelings** and our **intentions.**"

Clear signals

Puppies that live in a human household easily learn to read the body language of their family members and work out how to predict future behavior from their signals and actions. Because puppies are good at this, we can use this ability to communicate with them before we have taught them words. In a dog's world, staring or prolonged eye contact represents a threat or a challenge. Humans often look lovingly at their puppy, making prolonged eye contact and exposing the teeth by smiling. At first, puppies can feel threatened by this and may look away or appear worried. As long as you do not threaten your puppy by staring at him, he should soon learn that you mean no harm and will learn to look back at you without shyness.

▽ **"Are you friendly?"**
This puppy is not sure about an encounter and so is trying a rather stiff play-bow, but with all senses alert in case it does not go well.

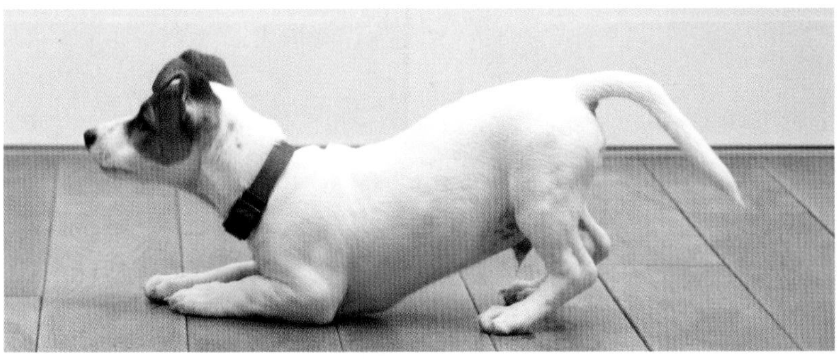

The **power** of **touch**

Dogs rarely touch or hold each other unless playing, fighting, or mating. Puppies need to become accustomed to being touched, held, and hugged by humans, and learn to enjoy and share this affection.

Safe hands

Puppies need to understand that being touched by humans is not harmful. In addition, it helps if they learn to enjoy our affectionate gestures, and they will be more successful pets if they are able to return this affection in a tactile way. Puppies also need to get used to being handled and restrained, both for general daily living and for veterinary treatment. If they get used to this early in their lives, they will be less likely to resist or be stressed when either handling or restraint is necessary.

The secret to good handling is to be gentle, but firm. Being hesitant or too rough, or accidently putting pressure on sensitive places, will cause your puppy to worry about being touched. Try to think what it feels like for him, and move your hands slowly, so that he has time to adjust to the new sensation. If your puppy starts to wriggle, make a conscious effort to slow your hands down, and move them over his body more slowly.

Sensitive areas

If you need to examine a sensitive area—such as the eyes, ears, face, whiskers, paws, or under the tail—and your puppy pulls away, try touching him close to that area instead. Reward calm acceptance with a tasty treat. Try again, slowly working your fingers gently toward

◁ **Up we go**
When lifting your puppy, hold him securely, lift slowly, and bring him to rest against you as soon as possible, so that he feels secure.

△ **Routine maintenance**
Use daily sessions to slowly get him used to procedures such as nail clipping, and even ear and hair plucking if his breed requires it.

◁ **Vet's exam**
Accustom your puppy to all the things a veterinarian will need to do while performing a routine examination, such as lifting the tail.

▷ **Teeth and mouth**
Begin getting your puppy used to having his mouth examined by lifting his lips, and over several sessions work toward opening his mouth.

the eyes or other sensitive area, and reward again for calm compliance. In this way, you can gradually work toward your goal, but give your puppy plenty of time for relaxation by massaging other areas of the body as well.

Many breeds require extensive grooming, so take advantage of these sessions and accustom your puppy to being groomed. Use brushes and combs that work for the length, type, and thickness of his hair, and groom small sections at a time. Get him used to having his back and sides brushed to start with, then slowly build up to grooming more sensitive areas, such as under the belly.

Restraint

As well as learning to accept being touched, your puppy will need to get used to being held and restrained. Hold him comfortably and securely, with all four feet on the ground at first. Your puppy will feel more secure if there is no chance of getting free, so restrain firmly, not holding him too tightly, but making sure that he cannot move around too much. Keep your hands underneath his chin if he tries to bite your fingers to get free. When you feel him begin to relax and accept the restraint, let your puppy go. Practice with short sessions, gradually holding him for longer periods each time. Your puppy will soon become comfortable with being held, and from there you can teach him to get used to being picked up. Do this by lifting him gently, and bring him in to your body so he is held securely.

> "The **secret** to **good handling** is to be **gentle, but firm.** Daily **sessions** will **help** your **puppy relax.**"

△ **Gentle massage**
Daily massage sessions will help your puppy to relax and learn to trust your touch, improving the relationship between you.

Getting used to clipping

Puppies with non-shed fur will need to be clipped later in life, often by professional groomers. This can be an ordeal for them, especially if they have not been accustomed to it from an early age. To prevent this from being an unpleasant experience, find some old electric clippers with the blades removed, and use these to get your puppy used to the noise and vibration. It is a good idea to take him to the groomers early in life so that he can get used to it.

What your puppy needs

A puppy can only be happy and well behaved if all its **needs** are **met**. Puppies that do not get enough food or exercise, or get too much play and too little sleep, are likely to be irritable, hyperactive, and prone to behavioral problems. This section explains **what makes puppies feel fulfilled**—from **love** and **attention** to clear **routines** and **good health**—and when you may need to seek **advice** from a professional. It also describes how your puppy may behave if he is getting too little or too much of something, so you can **recognize the signs** and **adjust things accordingly.**

HAPPY AND RELAXED
If all your puppy's physical and mental needs are satisfied, he will be happier and easier to live with as a puppy and as a full-grown dog.

Puppy essentials

Puppies have several important needs that must be met every day. As well as a good diet, they need a routine to follow, time to play, affection from their owners, regular exercise, and a chance to rest and sleep.

Love and attention

Puppies need plenty of affection and attention every day if they are to feel that they are part of the family. It is usually easy for owners to do this, but you may need to find regular slots in a packed schedule to sit down with your puppy and give him your undivided attention, especially if you have children and a busy family life. Puppies thrive on affection, and taking time to pet them and talk to them often throughout the day will make them better pets in years to come. Puppies that do not get enough attention will become clingy and demanding, and may also be hyperactive in their attempts to get someone to notice them.

Exercise

As well as affection, puppies need exercise to burn off energy. A safe area, away from traffic, where your puppy can run free is useful, although keeping a long line attached to your puppy's harness in an open area can fulfill the same purpose. It is important not to over-exercise puppies or take them on forced route marches where they have to walk long distances on a leash, since this can damage developing joints and bones. It is better to allow your puppy the freedom to exercise himself, as he will then stop naturally when he is tired. Puppies that don't get enough exercise will be over-exuberant and hyperactive. They will find it hard to concentrate on anything requiring their attention, and may also be boisterous in their frantic attempts to use up energy.

Playtime

Puppies need play to stimulate their development, to learn, and to use up physical and mental energy. Try to have short play and training sessions regularly throughout the

◁ **Routine matters**
A routine helps your puppy to adjust to your household and makes his life more predictable – useful at a time when he is having many new experiences.

▽ **Regular habits**
Regular feeding and other routines will make bathroom habits predictable and, as a result, it will be much easier to housebreak your puppy (pp.94–7).

△ **Using a leash**
Accustom your puppy to wearing a collar until he no longer notices it. Then attach a light leash, and hold it loosely or let it trail around after him.

△ **Having fun**
Make time for several short play sessions throughout the day. Play uses up lots of physical and mental energy, and results in a relaxed, contented, easygoing puppy.

day. This will keep your puppy busy and tire him, so he is more contented at home and less likely to get into mischief. Puppies that do not get much opportunity to play can become excessively inquisitive, and often get into trouble by being destructive around the house.

Sleep

Puppies need lots of sleep, especially when young. Lack of sleep will make them irritable. They can easily be encouraged to stay awake if something exciting is happening around them, but will soon get overtired and begin to feel unhappy. Make sure your puppy always has access to a comfortable, warm, and quiet place where he can sleep. In a busy household, it is a good idea to set nap times, and to put your puppy to bed to rest at regular intervals through the day.

△ **Out and about**
Once your puppy is fully vaccinated, taking him out to meet the world will help him socialize, as well as give him exercise.

Suggested routine for an 8-week-old puppy

8:00am	Wake up. Bathroom. Short play/training session.
9:00am	Puppy's breakfast.
9:15am	Bathroom. Short play/training session. Rest period.
10:00am	Bathroom. Exercise. Rest.
11:00am	Bathroom. Socialization time.
12:00pm	Bathroom.
1:00pm	Puppy's second meal.
1:15pm	Bathroom. Rest period.
2:00pm	Bathroom. Short play/training session. Rest period.
3:00pm	Bathroom. Socialization time.
4:00pm	Bathroom. Rest period.
5:00pm	Short play/training/exercise session. Puppy's third meal.
5:15pm	Bathroom. Rest period.
6:00pm	Bathroom. Play/training.
7:00pm	Bathroom. Rest period.
8:00pm	Handling/grooming session.
9:00pm	Puppy's fourth meal.
9:15pm	Bathroom. Training session.
10:00pm	Bathroom. Vigorous play.
11:00pm	Bathroom. Bed.

Health matters

Good health is important if your puppy is to grow and thrive. You need to know what to feed him, how to keep him healthy and protected, and how to find a good veterinarian.

Going to the vet

Before taking home your puppy, it is a smart idea to ask other dog owners in your area to recommend a good veterinarian. A particular veterinary practice should stand out, and you can then get in contact to register your new arrival. Good veterinarians and practices are worth holding on to, so take the time to develop a good relationship with the staff there, since this will make visits more successful for all of you—especially during any emergencies.

The veterinary practice will arrange an appointment for you to visit with your puppy once he has had a chance to settle into your household. He will then be checked by the veterinarian for any ailments, and whether he has been vaccinated, treated for fleas, and wormed. The practice will arrange for a second appointment for your puppy to receive the rest of his vaccinations, if required. Since the vet will know the prevalence of canine diseases in your local area, he or she will be the best person to advise you on how long it will be before your puppy is protected by vaccinations, and for how long you should keep him away from other unvaccinated dogs and places where they may have defecated.

The veterinary practice may also hold puppy playgroups or puppy parties. These provide a good chance for you to get to know the practice staff, and for your puppy to get used to going to the vet. The staff may encourage you to use the weighing scales and put your puppy on the examining table. This is all good experience for him and will make him less afraid of the vet's office later on. If staff members encourage puppy play, check that the play is between selected puppies and that it is carefully supervised. Unrestricted play in a free-for-all situation, where the puppies play together

△ **Enjoy the wait**
Use treats and praise to encourage your puppy to enjoy his time in the vet's waiting room, and to remove any apprehensions he may have.

▷ **Good experiences**
Early, positive encounters at the veterinarian can set your puppy up for a lifetime of stress-free trips to the vet.

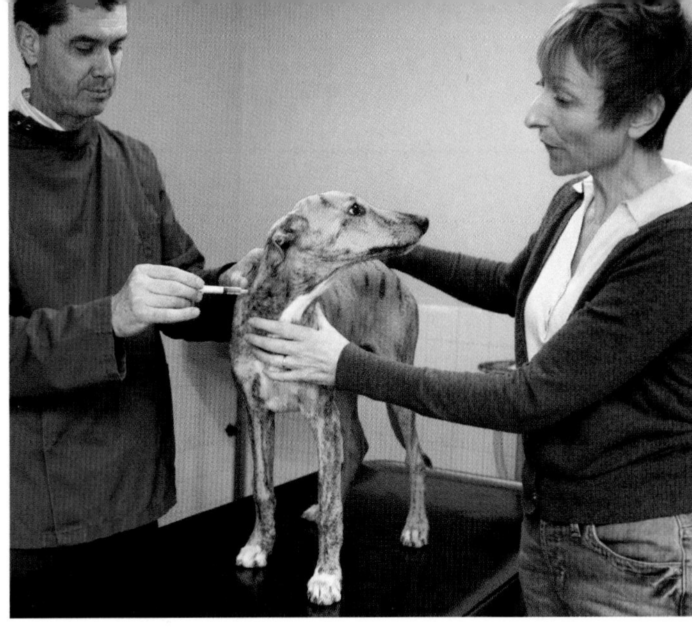

"Try to **develop** a good **rapport** with your local **veterinarian.**"

◁ **Thoughtful approach**
Finding a veterinarian who handles your puppy kindly will allow him to cope easily with the early experiences of treatment and examination.

without supervision for long periods, can do more harm than good, and may result in scared or aggressive puppies, or in puppies that learn to bully others.

Food and feeding

Make sure you feed your puppy the right quantity for his size, and increase his food allowance as he grows. This may seem obvious, but it is easy to forget to increase the amount you give him. If your puppy is underfed, he will be thin and often snappy around food, trying to get more to eat by snatching food from your fingers. He may also bite and mouth hands excessively, trying, in his own way, to persuade you to give him more to eat. Equally, do not be tempted to overfeed, but keep an eye on your puppy's weight to make sure he does not get fat. Ask your vet if you are unsure.

▷ **Pick it up**
Keep walking areas clean by picking up after your puppy. Use a strong plastic bag with your hand inside to keep it clean.

Types of food

There is now a vast array of different prepared foods for dogs and it is personal choice as to which one might be best. Be sure to choose a food that is specially formulated for puppies, so that it has all the nutrients your puppy requires to build a strong body. You will need to change to an adult formula as your puppy matures. Some people prefer to feed raw, natural food in the form of raw meat, bones, and pulverized vegetables rather than pre-packaged dog food.

Dry food for small puppies

Dry food for larger puppies

Raw food

Meat from a sachet

Canned food

3

Socialization

Learning to live in our world

Learning to live in our world

Socialization will have a tremendous **impact** on your puppy's **future behavior**, and can make all the difference between a shy, scared dog and an **outgoing, friendly, well-adjusted** one. Your new puppy will be living almost exclusively in a **world of humans**. This section tells you how to get him used to the **wide variety of people**, young and old, that he will **encounter** throughout his life, along with all the strange things they do. It also tells you how to **accustom your puppy** to the **sights, scents, and sounds** that surround humans, and to other dogs and **different animals.**

SCARY WORLD
Gradually get your puppy used to everyday objects, such as noisy vacuum cleaners, so he grows up to be confident in the human world.

Socialization with humans

Getting socialization right is critical for breeders and owners. It should be done carefully, paying special attention to getting the puppy used to all types and ages of people.

Why socialize?

Puppies are born with no knowledge of the world, and gradually have to learn what is safe and what is not. Their innate fear of new things is suspended for a short time (see panel, right) while they get used to their new environment. Once this window closes, their wariness of new things keeps them safe from hazards they may encounter later in life. While this works well in the wild, it is more of a hindrance in a human world. We take responsibility for keeping our puppies safe, and having a puppy who is afraid of ordinary things and events is hard for us and stressful for the puppy.

To prevent puppies from becoming fearful, they need to be acclimatized at a young age to all the things they may face later. This means an intensive period of socialization during the first year of a puppy's life, and a concerted effort from both breeder and new owner.

Good socialization

Good socialization is done at a speed the puppy can handle. Watch your puppy's body language (pp.66–7) and make sure he is enjoying the experience. Allow plenty of time for rest, so that his brain can take in all that it has learned. Your puppy should have daily socialization sessions, ideally several times a day. Take him out with you and expose him to more and more as he learns to cope with it. Shy puppies, especially those not socialized by the breeder, will need a lot more work to help them become well adjusted (pp.86–7).

Meeting people

Puppies need to get used to all kinds of people. Babies, toddlers, and teenagers are very different

△ **Happy encounter**
The easiest way to socialize your puppy is to take him out to meet your friends in different environments, and invite people to your house.

▷ **Overwhelming**
Encounters should not be worrying. This shy puppy is overwhelmed by the man looming over him with full eye contact.

▷ **Socializing opportunity**
Try to make encounters fun, with toys and treats. Walk your puppy away if he isn't enjoying it.

▽ **Making friends**
Pay special attention to helping your puppy have fun with children of all ages, especially if there are no children in your family.

> **"Puppies** need to be **acclimatized** at a **young age** to all the things they may **encounter later."**

from one another. Some people will be overpowering, others gentle. Puppies need to learn from an early age to take everyone in their stride, and owners should make a special effort to help their puppy make as many human friends as possible during puppyhood. Getting used to different people in a wide variety of environments will help to increase your puppy's understanding, and his confidence in strange situations and tolerance of new things will slowly increase.

▷ **Big wide world**
Carry your puppy out to see the world until his vaccinations have taken effect, getting him used to different places and situations.

Timing

Breeders and owners need to take advantage of the window of opportunity when a puppy is still young enough not to fear new experiences.

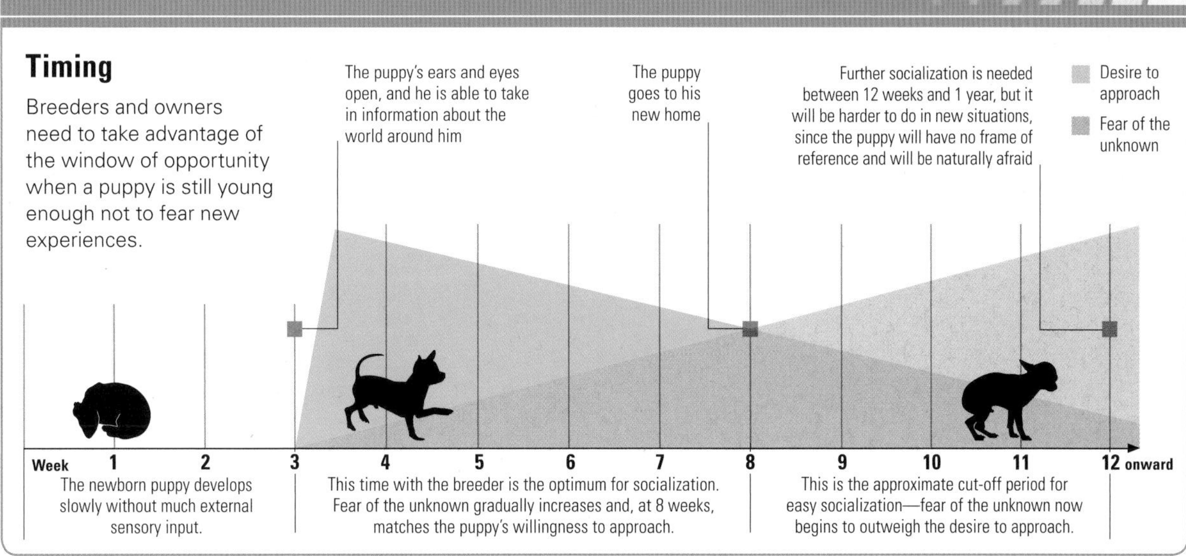

Your **puppy** and **other animals**

Puppies have to get used to other animals, and not just humans. Not only must they learn to interact well with other puppies and dogs, they also need to learn to tolerate other species, such as cats, rabbits, and horses.

Other dogs

Your puppy's education about other dogs needs to continue after he has left the litter. It is essential that he has encounters with as many carefully chosen dogs and puppies as possible while he is still a puppy. This will help him to learn the social skills and body language necessary for friendly encounters when he is older (pp.104–5). The more social skills your puppy acquires at a young age, the better he will be able to deflect conflicts and avoid aggressive encounters with other dogs.

For socialization with other dogs to work well, the dogs your puppy meets need to be non-aggressive. An encounter with a dog that is aggressive to him, or even just too boisterous, can leave mental scars that may result in your puppy being aggressive to other dogs later in life, especially if he has a nervous disposition. Keep him away from unfamiliar dogs and stop aggressive encounters immediately, making up for them later with friendly meetings with similar types of dogs in a comparable environment.

Try to find adult dogs that are used to puppies and have a relaxed, friendly temperament around other dogs. A small circle of friendly doggy friends is better than a wider circle that includes aggressive

△ **Perfect playtimes**
Make sure puppy play is controlled and supervised and all puppies are relaxed and having fun, rather than a free-for-all where some puppies are scared or overwhelmed.

"Try to find **adult dogs** that are used to puppies and that have a **relaxed, friendly disposition.**"

▷ **Approach with caution**
It is not always easy to know which dogs will be tolerant of puppies, so it is wise to keep your puppy away from dogs you are not sure about.

◁ **Meeting rabbits**
Recognizing the rabbit as one of the family, this puppy play-bows to encourage play. Keep encounters calm to prevent your puppy from scaring the rabbit.

△ **"What are you?"**
Encounters with animals that could harm or frighten your puppy need care—keep your distance to ensure safety and a good experience.

dogs. Even so, the more canine friends your puppy has and the more time he spends with them, the better he will be at dealing with other dogs in the future.

It is not enough for your puppy to interact only with one other dog at home. To be well socialized he needs to have encounters with many different shapes and sizes of dog, with varying temperaments.

Puppies

It is usually easier to find other puppies for your puppy to play with than it is to find older dogs. You may decide to go to puppy parties at the veterinarian or puppy classes where there is controlled play. It is important that your puppy does not get overwhelmed during these encounters, and you need to intervene if you think he is getting bullied or is becoming stressed (pp.104–5).

Other animals

If you have a cat at home and you help your puppy build a happy, respectful relationship with it, he will be nicer to cats he encounters in the future, and less likely to chase cats when away from home, especially if the breeder had cats too. If not, try to find cats that will not run away and gently acclimatize your puppy to their presence from a distance.

Gradually getting your puppy used to horses and livestock is necessary if you want your puppy to accept them readily in the future. Make sure these encounters are calm, with no chasing possible.

▷ **Sheep encounter**
Use a barrier to ensure your puppy is not worried about the sheep if they decide to approach, and a leash to help you prevent your puppy from chasing or scaring them.

"More play now?"
The Collie puppy (left) is lively and ready to resume his active play session with the Spaniel (right). But the Spaniel is still resting, so he tries to avoid the Collie's gaze in order to avoid being jumped on.

Help for **shy puppies**

A shy puppy needs help to overcome his worries and develop into a confident dog. If no one does this or recognizes his fears, he may grow up to be nervous and aggressive.

Why be shy?

Puppies do not need to have bad experiences to make them shy and afraid. Lack of experience or socialization at an appropriate time, particularly in the early weeks when they are with the breeder (pp.16–17), combined with a nervous disposition, can cause puppies to be timid and worried about new encounters. Some dogs are genetically prone to being scared, such as many herding breeds, and these dogs will need earlier and better socialization than dogs of other breeds that are more mentally robust.

Owners of shy puppies will need to work hard in the early weeks to help their puppies overcome their fears without overwhelming them, particularly if the cause of the shyness was lack of socialization by the breeder. Signs of improvement will gradually become evident as the puppy grows. Failure to deal with the problem at the right time will result in permanent shyness, and may even lead to your puppy becoming aggressive later, once he reaches maturity and becomes more confident.

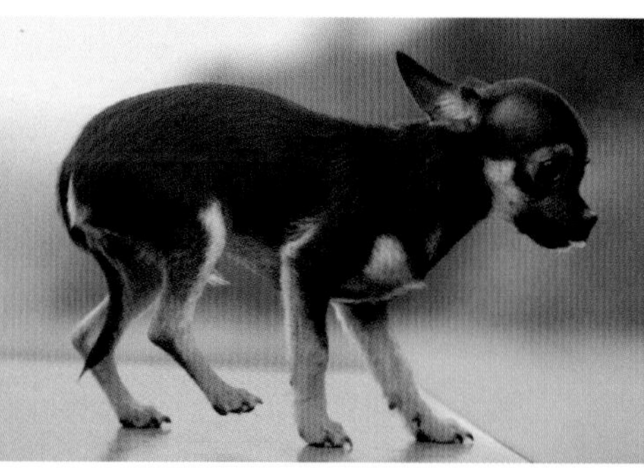

▷ **So scared**
This Chihuahua is exhibiting all the signs of fear—tail down, ears back, hunched posture, big eyes, tongue flicking in and out. When you see this, help your puppy out.

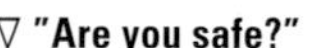

▽ **"Are you safe?"**
Uncertain whether the big sheep is safe to approach or not, this puppy keeps his weight on his back legs, ready to run.

△ **Safety zone**
Keeping your distance from things that frighten your puppy can help him learn to relax. Imagine a circle of safety around your puppy and move away from the object of fear, if necessary.

"**You** will **need many sessions with** a **shy puppy** to help him get **over** his **fears.**"

Taking action

If your puppy is timid or worried about certain things, think ahead to try to prevent him from getting scared. Create a safety zone around him to keep him at a distance at which he feels comfortable, and try not to allow unexpected encounters within that safety zone, especially when he is on a leash and cannot get away. This distance will help your puppy feel safe, and you will be able to work on the problem more easily at your convenience.

As often as you can, do small sessions to help your puppy overcome his fears. Practice getting as close as you can to whatever he is afraid of, but watch his body language carefully for any signs of fear—for example, tail down, ears back, yawning, wide eyes, intense stare. If you begin to see any of these signs, move back a little and go less far next time. Then spend time at this distance, playing with your puppy, helping him to relax and have fun, and feeding him tasty treats. If he cannot relax, move farther back. Once he is playing happily, move a little closer and try again. Always finish on a good note and walk away.

You will need to do lots of these sessions in order for your puppy to conquer his fears, each time getting a tiny bit closer. It is certainly worth doing though, and will make all the difference to the future welfare and happiness of both you and your puppy. If he has more than one fear, concentrate on the easiest first, and gradually work up to tackling the more difficult ones.

It may also be useful to purchase a product called Dog Appeasing Pheromone from your veterinarian. This product simulates the safe smell of the canine mother, and has proven very useful in helping scared and shy puppies to overcome their fears.

▷ **In hiding**
The Collie puppy is worried by the presence of this interested, confident older dog, and so hides behind his owner's legs, licking his nose to calm himself down.

Habituation

The process of getting puppies used to non-living things and acclimatizing them to all the sights, smells, sounds, and events that are a part of our modern world is known as habituation.

Getting used to things

To be successful pets, puppies must take all the things that happen in the normal world of humans in their stride and not be afraid of them. Getting used to these things in a gradual way so they learn to accept them is an important part of puppyhood. If habituation is not done well, you may end up with a fearful, reactive dog that is stressed throughout its life and difficult for you to control.

◁ **Monstrous machines**
This puppy has gradually become accustomed to the washing machine, but puppies can be scared of machines they haven't encountered before.

At home

Although we take our home and everything in it for granted, it can seem like a very scary place to a new puppy, unless he was raised in a home environment by the breeder. To overcome this, watch your puppy carefully for signs of distress. If he is shy, take things slowly and help him to overcome his fears (pp.84–5).

Outside

The outside world can be much more challenging for a young puppy. If your puppy is very young and not yet vaccinated, take him outside but hold him in your arms. In this way, he can get used to all the sights and smells of the outside world from a safe position and will be better prepared for walks later.

Once your puppy has been vaccinated, take him out as much as possible. Start slowly and be careful not to overwhelm him with too much, too soon. Remember how small he is and how vulnerable he may feel. Go at his speed, gently

▽ **Noisy pans**
Even the everyday noise of pans and dishes crashing and banging in the kitchen can be too much for your puppy if he is not used to it.

> "Although we take the **appliances** in our **homes** for **granted,** they can seem **scary** to a **new puppy.**"

▷ **Road traffic**
Take your puppy to places where you can sit back from the road and gradually let him get used to vehicles passing by.

protecting him from unpleasant encounters. Take special care to introduce him to car travel, so he becomes a good passenger (pp.122–3). Gradually get him used to all the things he will encounter on the streets, in parks, and in the countryside, such as people walking down the street wearing backpacks, children riding bicycles, livestock in the country, and large vehicles on busy roads.

It is not difficult to habituate your puppy to all the things he needs to get used to in life, but you do need to think and act while he is still young.

△ **Confident puppy**
If your puppy has been raised well by the breeder he should be able to take most things in his stride. Shy puppies will need much more help.

Loud noises

It is important to get your puppy used to loud sounds, such as the bang of fireworks, from an early age. CDs of various sudden-onset noises are commercially available, so you can desensitize your puppy gradually at home. Start at a very low volume. Turn up the noise a bit and offer games and treats, but turn the sound down if your puppy is startled. Turn off and repeat. Keep sessions short, and slowly increase the volume over many sessions. To cope with unexpected loud noises, act jolly, as if they are of no concern, and lead your puppy away.

△ **Scary scales**
A friendly veterinarian and a kind approach will help your puppy learn to trust and accept machines and procedures at the vet's.

4

Essential lessons

Housebreaking

One of the most important lessons for a young puppy is learning how to be clean in the house. Puppies naturally **keep their nest clean**, unless they have been raised in dirty conditions. All we need to do is help them understand that **our whole house is their nest**, and so they must **go outside if they want to relieve themselves**. It is normal for your puppy to have a few **accidents** at first, but if you **know what to do** and are there at the **right times** to do it, he will learn more quickly. The **keys** to effective housebreaking are **supervision, consistency, persistence, and sticking to a routine**. Follow the guidelines in this section to **achieve success.**

END RESULT
Encouraging your puppy to go to the bathroom outside is simple, providing you watch him closely in the early weeks.

How to **housebreak**

Housebreaking is easy once you know exactly what to do, but you will need to make an effort. Constant surveillance and taking your puppy outside at appropriate times are essential.

Successful technique

When puppies need to relieve themselves, they will naturally search for the type of surface they have been used to going on. This means that puppies that have been raised in a house and taken outside by the breeder to go on the grass will be virtually housebroken when they arrive. In contrast, if your puppy has learned to go on the concrete floor of a kennel, he will search for a hard surface, such as your kitchen floor, and you will have to convince him to go to the bathroom on the grass instead.

When your puppy is very young and has just arrived home, it is a good idea for one person to take charge of his housebreaking. Alternatively, carefully take turns keeping track of him. Your puppy will need to be taken out at the following times:

- After feeding or drinking.
- After sleeping.
- After playing.
- After any excitement, such as when visitors arrive.
- If he looks like he is about to go—common signs include sniffing intently, circling, or a faraway expression.
- Every hour if none of the above has happened.

Supervise your puppy at all times when he is in the house, and invite him outside if you think he needs to go. When you cannot watch him, take him outside, play a short game with him, and encourage him to go into his playpen with a chew. Do not leave him in the pen for more than an hour before taking him out to relieve himself and for exercise.

△ **Be vigilant**
Being too busy to concentrate on your puppy may lead to accidents in the house, which will set your housebreaking program back.

◁ **Be patient**
Stay outside with your puppy, or he will try to get back into the house to be with you, and will need to go to the bathroom again once inside.

Nighttime

At night, take your puppy to your bedroom until he has learned to be left alone (pp.58–9). You will then hear when he wakes up, and you can take him outside to go to the bathroom. If you are vigilant, your puppy will learn to be clean more quickly, and will be housebroken by the time you move him out of your bedroom to sleep. If you must leave him alone at night, listen carefully for times when he wakes up, and rush to let him outside.

How long?

Some puppies learn more quickly than others. With your undivided attention, it should be possible to establish a housebreaking routine, so that your puppy does not have any accidents in the house after the first week. Otherwise, if your housebreaking routing is sporadic, it could take several months for him to be fully housebroken.

△ **No accidents**
Leave your puppy in the playpen for no more than an hour, and when you let him out of the pen, take him outside right away.

Keep it positive

If your puppy has an accident in the house, consider it to be your fault for not supervising him correctly, and make every effort to ensure that it does not happen again. If you punish your puppy for having an accident inside, he will learn to avoid you when he needs to go, and will develop a habit of sneaking off to do it when your back is turned, which will make it much more difficult to housebreak him. Give him lots of praise when he goes in the right place, and move him out to the backyard if he is in the wrong place. He will soon get the idea.

▷ **Keep it up**
Puppies will not be fully housebroken until they are about 6 months of age, so keep inviting your puppy out when you think he needs to go.

▽ **All weathers**
Go outside with your puppy whatever the weather, so that he gets into good habits and no longer needs you to be close by when he goes.

Housebreaking problems

Housebreaking a puppy is not always straightforward, especially when the puppy has been raised in less than ideal conditions. Do not despair if you are struggling with the training—you will succeed eventually.

Dirty conditions

Puppies brought up in very dirty conditions, or where there is no distinction between the area where they sleep and the area in which they play and relieve themselves, are likely to be difficult to housebreak. Most puppies will not go to the bathroom where they sleep, but puppies raised in grimy conditions learn not to care, and will stop and go wherever they are. If your puppy is indiscriminate in this way, make an intensive effort to keep him with you at all times. Watch him carefully, so you can help him when he needs to go by rapidly taking him to the correct place. One way to keep an eye on him is to attach a line to his collar and fasten the other end to your belt, so that it acts as an umbilical cord between the two of you.

△ **Hard surfaces**
Puppies raised on concrete by the breeder will search out hard surfaces, such as kitchen floors and patios, to go to the bathroom.

Bathroom preferences

Housebreaking will be more difficult if your puppy has already learned to go on a type of surface that is different from the surface you want him to use. For example, he may have learned to go on concrete instead of grass, or he may prefer grass when you would prefer him to go to the bathroom on concrete. If your puppy was not supervised well by the breeder at a very young age, he may even have already learned to go on the carpet.

Solving this problem will require vigilance and perseverance. During the first week of housebreaking when you are making an intensive effort (pp.94–5), make sure you keep your puppy away from his preferred surface at any time when he is likely to go—for example, after eating or sleeping—and only give him access to places where you want him to go. This can be difficult at first, as he may try to hold on until he can use his "bathroom," but if you persist, he

△ **Litter training**
The litter box should be large with low sides. Persuade your puppy to use it at bathroom times, or if you see him starting to go elsewhere, by encouraging him to get into it.

△ **Familiar smell**
Once your puppy has learned to go in the litter box, try taking some soiled litter outside and putting it down on the grass. This will help him learn to go there as well.

“**Make** an **intensive effort** during **the first few weeks,** and **your puppy** will soon **learn new habits.**”

will soon learn new habits. Using the umbilical method of attaching your puppy to you, as described above, may also help.

No backyard

If you have a puppy of a small breed and no backyard, it may suit you to train him to use a litter box similar to one a cat would use. It is harder to teach this method than it is to train your puppy to use the yard, since he will not be able to run around and sniff first—which helps to stimulate a puppy to go—but it is possible with perseverance.

To start the process, encourage your puppy to investigate the box filled with litter. Get him used to jumping in and out without concern. Then take him to the box whenever you think he needs to go or has just started to go. Be patient, since this not a simple process, and it is easy to get frustrated with lack of progress and accidents. You may find it helpful, to start with, to use puppy pads, which are available commercially and impregnated with a scent that encourages their use. Lay the pads out across a wide area, and gradually reduce the size of this area as your puppy begins to use them. Eventually, when he is using just one pad, place it in the litter box to encourage him to go there. Once he has learned to use the box, you may want to teach him to go on grass as well. To do this, place some of his soiled litter on the grass to help him to understand that his bathroom is there, too.

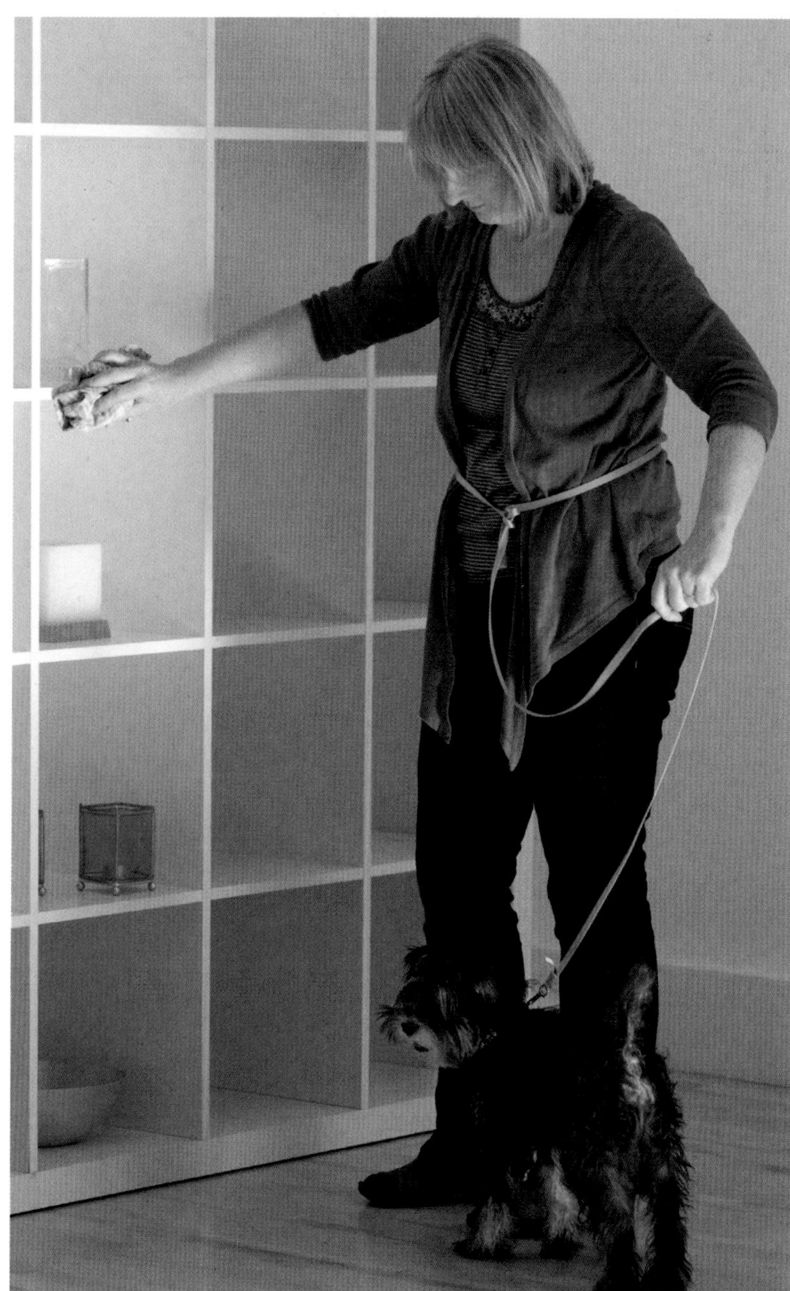

△ **Umbilical method**
Use a line to keep your puppy close to you. This way, you are constantly reminded to check what he is doing before you move away from him.

Additional help

If you cannot train your puppy to be clean and are still struggling after 2 weeks of intensive effort, get him checked out by your veterinarian in case there is something wrong. Your vet will also be able to refer you to an experienced behaviorist or trainer who will help you further.

Playtime

Puppies love to play, and owners can use this **natural** behavior to their advantage by using playtimes to teach their puppies how to have fun with people. A **well-adjusted dog** will **enjoy playing with humans**, but at the same time it will take care not to be too boisterous or accidentally bite skin instead of a toy. Follow the **guidelines** in this section to teach your puppy how to play **different types of games with toys**, and you will find him easier to handle if he gets excited. In addition, **supervising play with other dogs** will mean that **humans take priority** in your puppy's mind, and he will happily **leave the other dogs to come to you**.

GOOD RELATIONSHIPS
Play strengthens the bonds between a puppy and his family. Continue to play with your dog once he reaches adulthood.

Play biting

Play biting is a puppy's way of playing with his littermates. Unless we teach our puppies how to play successfully with us using toys, they will direct their play bites onto us instead.

Causes and solutions

Puppies learn to play in their litter by biting and mouthing other puppies. When they do the same to us, it hurts, since they have sharp puppy teeth and we have no fur to protect us. Even if we express disapproval, they are so desperate to play after being separated from their litter that they try their hardest to get us to play in the only way they know.

To stop your puppy from play biting, you need to teach him how to play with you using toys instead. Start with fluffy, soft toys—ideally about the same size as a small puppy—because these simulate your puppy's brothers and sisters. This makes it easier for him to understand what to do. Then follow the procedure described on pages 102–5. To start with, make sure you have a toy with you whenever you interact with your puppy. Use it to stop him biting you, by moving the toy around close to his mouth so that he bites on it instead of you.

If your puppy accidentally forgets and bites your hands or feet instead, stand up, taking the toy with you, and keep still. Do not look at him or talk to him until all excitement has subsided, and he has wandered off.

Extreme play biting

If your puppy bites hard or your skin is easily damaged, or you have young children in the house who are frightened by his play biting, you will need to maintain a greater level of control until he has learned to put his teeth only on toys. To achieve this, attach a long line to his collar. This will help you restrict his range, and allow you to put only the toy within the reach of his mouth and puppy teeth.

▷ **Ouch!**
Puppies are not being aggressive when they play bite—they are simply inviting us to play in a way that humans often do not understand.

▽ **Fluffy substitute**
Encourage your puppy to play with a large toy, rather than biting your fingers. He will soon begin to focus play on to toys instead.

Why play?

Play is a very important part of life for dogs of all ages. It gives them an outlet for their energy, and is a good substitute for all the behavior normally associated with catching prey. Playing with toys is fun once a dog has learned how to do it, and it is a good way to give your dog plenty of exercise. It also helps build a good relationship between you and your puppy, and if you teach him rules to games (pp.102–5), you will be much more able to stay in control of him in times of excitement. Adult dogs need to play just as much as puppies, so do not stop once your puppy has matured.

Successful toys

Puppies need different types of toys at different times in their lives. While still very young and teething, they will need large, soft, fluffy toys that resemble their littermates. As they grow, learn to play with people, and acquire a full set of adult teeth, they can be given soft toys that are more robust and include ropes and other hard parts. As puppies mature into adults, you can substitute harder balls and ropes for the soft toys.

Toys for very young puppies

Toys for older puppies

Toys for adult dogs

△ **Game over**
If your puppy play bites you, take the toy away and ignore your puppy—this will teach him to be more careful with his teeth the next time.

▷ **Careful supervision**
Use a line to ensure your puppy bites only the toy until he is more experienced. Remove the line before leaving him unsupervised.

Successful playtimes

Getting play right is important, because both you and your puppy need to enjoy it to do it well. You need just the right combination of fun and control for playtimes to be a success.

How to play

With a very young puppy, you will need a large, soft toy (p.101), which is big enough to avoid him accidentally catching your fingers when he grabs it. Get down to your puppy's level and move the toy around erratically, sometimes slow, sometimes fast, sometimes around your body so that it disappears and then appears again. Try not to be too competitive, keeping the toy to yourself all the time. Instead, let your puppy get it sometimes, and let him try to pull it away from you while you hold it and pull gently back occasionally. Every so often, throw the toy for him, but be careful not to throw it too high or he will wonder where it has gone and lose interest.

Sometimes let your puppy take the toy away, and be patient until he brings it back to you for another game. If he drops it, run over to the toy and encourage him to pick it up. Praise your puppy warmly when he is holding it and pet his sides, rather than his head, so that he does not learn to avoid you when he has the toy, thinking you are going to take it away. This will make teaching him the retrieve easier later (pp.164–5).

Try to make games fun and never get frustrated if your puppy will not play. If he is not interested, concentrate on the game rather than him, and try to show him how much fun you are having so that he wants to join in. Finish before either of you has had enough. In

△ **Irresistible**
The toy will be most enticing to your puppy if it resembles a fast-moving animal wriggling in and out of cover. Keep it moving erratically to encourage a pounce.

▷ **Flying fox**
Try throwing the toy a short distance, so that your puppy can chase it down, but keep it in his line of vision, otherwise he will wonder where it has gone.

△ **Chase games**
Some dogs prefer the thrill of the chase, whereas others enjoy the feeling of possession when they catch the toy, making it difficult to get the toy back again.

△ **Pulling contest**
Tug-of-war is the favorite game of many dogs—especially competitive dogs—as they enjoy the energy release and feelings of strength and competition that the game evokes.

> **"Try to make games fun and never get frustrated if your puppy will not play."**

this way, you will encourage great enthusiasm for games with toys, which will give you a good foundation for later training and exercise. Take away soft toys at the end of the game so that your puppy does not destroy them, but leave him toys that are more robust, so that he has something to play with and chew when he is by himself.

As your puppy grows and learns more about how to play with toys and with humans, you will soon recognize the types of game he likes to play. He may prefer tug-of-war games, squeaky toy games, or chase games. Playing games together regularly will help you learn about each other's strengths, skills, and capabilities.

Controlling games

Games need rules if they are to be successful for both owner and puppy. Make sure your puppy learns to bite on the toy instead of hands (pp.100–1), and learns to stop and give up the toy when asked—offer a toy or a treat instead and pair with a cue, so he figures out that he has to drop on cue (pp.142–3). He also needs to learn to wait until he is offered the toy before starting to play. To do this, keep the toy out of reach, and wait until he is sitting before throwing it. Teaching good manners during games will mean that your puppy can play with anyone, including children, without accidentally hurting them. Later, you can also train him to wait while a toy is thrown (pp.166–7) and a chase recall (pp.170–1), so that he learns to be fully under control, even at times of excitement.

▷ **In control**
If you can control your puppy when he is energized at the thought of playing games, you are more likely to be in control at other times of high excitement.

Play with **other dogs**

Carefully supervising play with other dogs when your puppy is very young will help you to ensure that he grows up being friendly with other dogs, and has the social skills to deflect hostile encounters.

Choosing playmates

Puppies benefit from playing with other sociable dogs, as this helps them pick up much-needed social skills. Even so, your puppy should still spend more time playing with people than with other dogs, since it is essential that he learns how to enjoy playing with you (pp.102–3).

During puppyhood, your puppy will need to meet and play with several adult dogs and puppies every week. All of the other dogs involved need to be friendly, sociable, and gentle in play. If your puppy plays with rough players and bullies and gets scared as a result, it may lead to problems later on (pp.82–3). Similarly, if you let him encounter dogs that behave in an aggressive manner toward him, you risk him becoming aggressive toward other dogs. Choosing who he plays with, how he plays with them, and for how long, will make all the difference in how your puppy behaves later.

△ **Saying hello**
Choose sociable dogs that are gentle with other dogs and make sure they have a proven track record of being friendly with puppies.

Protect your puppy from unwanted encounters with unknown dogs in the park by keeping your distance. If an unknown dog runs up, command it to "sit" as it approaches, and throw a handful of treats in its direction. This may distract it long enough for you to make an escape.

Supervising puppy play

Keep a careful watch and stop games if it looks like things are getting out of hand. Do not allow your puppy to do anything to the other dog that will not be acceptable when your puppy is older. Stop him if he grabs and

> "Your **puppy** should **meet and play** with other **puppies** and **dogs** every week."

◁ **Firm friends**
For each 5-minute play session your puppy has with other dogs, you need to have three 5-minute sessions with him, so he stays human-focused.

◁ **Stay with me**
Making sure your puppy prefers games with toys with you to natural games with other dogs will ensure you can get him back from other dogs during a walk.

shakes the other dog, or tries to pin him down, or climbs on his back. If you see your puppy doing any of these things, gently move him with your hands or hold him and turn him away, allowing him to calm down before he goes back to the game. Stop games if either dog looks worried and tries to get away.

Puppies, like young children, tire quickly. Keep play sessions shorter than 10 minutes for older puppies, and less than 4 minutes for very young puppies. They can have additional sessions later, once they have had a rest.

△ **Well matched**
Ideally your puppy's playmates should be of a similar age and size, so they do not overpower him in play or allow him to win wrestling matches too often.

The right balance

It is important not to let your puppy play doggy games constantly. If you do, your puppy will grow up being very dog-focused, learning mostly from other dogs, taking more notice of them and ignoring you. Your puppy should play with humans for three times as long as he plays with other dogs. This way, he will grow up being people-focused and will be a much more successful pet as a result.

▽ **Time for a break**
If your puppy needs a rest and the other dog is non-aggressive, crouch down, bring your puppy in between your legs, and fend off the other dog.

Chewing

Puppies often get into trouble for chewing, even though it is **normal puppy behavior**. The **destruction of household items** is a nuisance, and can be expensive. If you are able to give your puppy **enough things to chew** and get him into **good habits from an early age**, there is no reason why he should chew your possessions. This section will help you **understand** the **different stages of chewing**, and why puppies chew during these times—so you can **ensure that your puppy chews only what he is supposed to**. It also offers tips on **what to give your puppy** to chew and how to **keep him interested** in what you are providing.

INEDIBLE
Puppies need safe, hard chews to use their teeth on. Soft toys will disintegrate if chewed, and may harm your puppy if swallowed.

The puppy chewing stage

Puppies need to chew and will do so voraciously while they are teething up until adolescence. Puppyhood is a good time to teach them what to chew on (and what not to), and to get them into good habits.

Why puppies chew

Puppies chew for two reasons: firstly, to relieve the discomfort caused during teething, when their puppy teeth are replaced by adult teeth—this happens between 3 and 6 months of age—and secondly, during exploration, when they pick up and touch things with their mouths in the same way that toddlers explore using their hands. They will continue to chew a great deal until they are about 6 months old, after which time the chewing slows down a little.

Good habits

It is important to get your puppy into good habits right away, rather than allowing him to learn to chew household items. Buy a variety of different chews so that you have plenty to offer at times when it is likely he will want to chew. Replace these frequently with a new selection throughout his puppyhood until he is at least a year old. Your puppy will be most likely to chew when he is rested and looking for something to do, or settling down to relax after a meal. Always have a different chew ready

△ Strong chews
Hide chews are made from dried skin and are well accepted by puppies. Soak the ends in water for a short time to soften them.

> **"Get him** into **good habits, rather than** allowing him to **chew household items."**

◁ Wide variety
Many chew toys reduce the risk to household furnishings. If you allow your puppy to mouth safe items, he is less likely to swallow harmful objects accidentally.

Chews for puppies

The best chews are firm but strong, yielding to young teeth, yet providing some resistance to strengthen jaws and massage gums. Safe chews do not easily disintegrate to leave sharp or indigestible pieces if swallowed. Do not give your puppy cooked bones, since they can splinter.

Wide variety
Chews sold in pet stores usually vary between strong rubber toys that can be stuffed with food, rawhide chews, and bones.

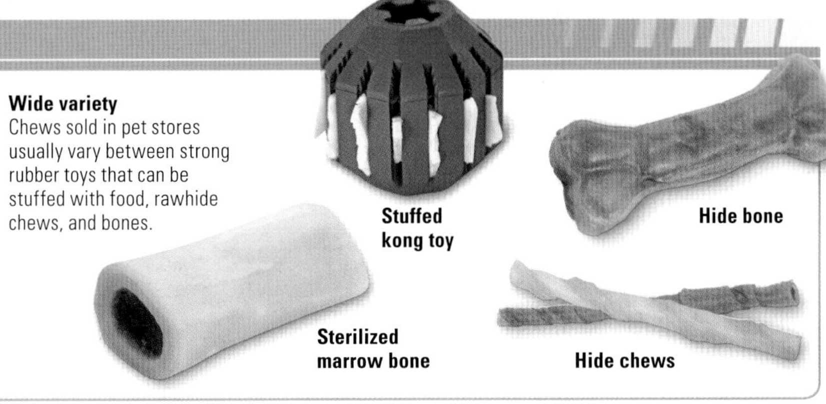

from the one he was chewing previously, and make sure he begins to chew it rather than a household item before you move away. If you cannot supervise your puppy, put him into his playpen with his chew, along with several other chews of a different variety, so that you know he does not have access to anything he should not chew.

Puppies can become very texture-specific when chewing, which means that they will try to return to items made from a certain type of material, such as wood, once they have learned how good it feels to chew. To counter this, keep your puppy far away from anything made out of this substance in the house, and instead offer him safe chews made from a material that is a suitable substitute.

If you see your puppy chewing a household item, distract him, and lead him away with a chew instead. Praise him gently when he settles down to chew it. If he is not interested in the chew and tries to return to what he was doing, give him a different chew, or try squeezing some tasty treats into the end of the chew.

◁ **Quiet time**
Chews provide an invaluable means of keeping your puppy occupied when you are busy or when you want to teach him to settle down. Keep back some special chews that he really likes for this purpose.

Averting accidents

Most owners expect young puppies to chew, and are happy to accept the occasional chewing accident. Even so, you can keep this to a minimum if you know what to do and you supervise your puppy constantly, putting him into his playpen when you are not able to do so. Pick up all loose household items, such as children's toys and remote controls, so that he is not tempted. Offer him a variety of chews, leaving some on the floor for him, and pick these up and put new ones down often. In addition, by keeping him busy with plenty of play sessions, games, and training, he will have limited energy left to chew household items.

▽ **Teething solutions**
Strong toys filled with food can be chilled to provide a cool soother for a teething puppy, or an interesting plaything and chew when you have to leave your puppy alone.

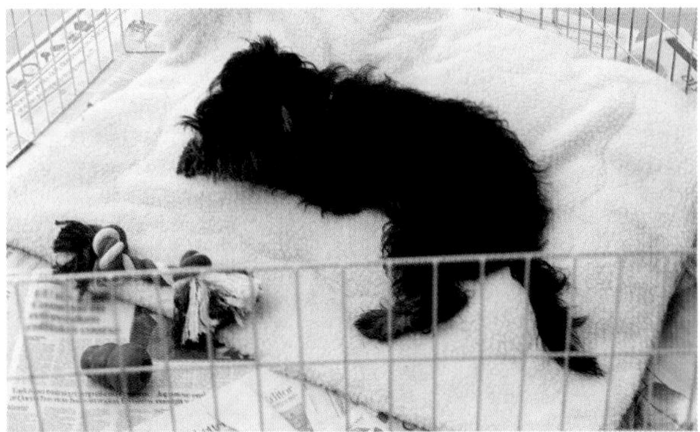

Adolescent chewing

During adolescence, your dog will be able to cause more damage when he chews than he could as a young puppy. It is essential that you understand why he does it, and make sure that he only chews appropriate items.

Timing

Adolescence begins at around 6 months. The adolescent chewing phase begins a little later, at about 7–9 months, and continues until the puppy is physically mature, at about 1 year old. At this age, the puppy is larger, with stronger jaws, and so can do more damage.

◁ **Kept in**
Confinement in the house for long periods can make an adolescent puppy frustrated and destructive as he tries to release energy.

Causes

It is likely that adolescent puppies need to chew to strengthen their jaws and teeth. In a natural habitat, this would coincide with a time when puppies would leave their mother and littermates and go off to explore on their own. During this time, they are programmed to travel long distances and to be on the move for most of the day. When we confine our puppies to a house, especially if they are left alone a lot or not exercised well, they may direct this active exploratory behavior toward household possessions and fixtures, with devastating results. Dogs bred to use their mouths—for example, Labradors—seem to be more prone to this behavior than others.

> "Before leaving your **puppy alone** at **home,** make sure you **pick up** loose **household items.**"

Solutions

If you are to keep your possessions safe during this time, it is essential that you provide your adolescent

▽ **Chewing challenge**
Exciting puzzles, like working out how to retrieve treats from a plastic bottle, use up energy and reduce the desire for exploration.

Time to explore

Adolescence is a time for exploration and discovery. Taking your puppy out and about to investigate—especially to places where he has never been before—will help satisfy his need to find out what is out there. If you do not do this, and instead confine him to the house, you may find that he tries to explore on a smaller scale, by investigating different things around the house with his teeth.

◁ **New pastures**
Adolescent puppies like to leave familiar places and explore. Being able to learn about new areas will make your puppy more contented at home.

puppy with plenty of different things to chew. Make sure the chews are large enough to keep him entertained for some time, and give him several at once if you have to leave him alone. If you have to leave your puppy again the next day, take these chews away and give him different ones.

As an extra precaution, try to leave your puppy with several puzzle feeders. For example, try cutting a few holes in a cardboard box and placing some tasty, smelly treats inside. Hide his dinner in stuffed toys, and be as inventive as you can to give him things to keep him occupied while you are out. He may have outgrown his puppy playpen by this stage, so keep him in a place where he is comfortable, but where he can do least damage. Pick up all loose household items before leaving your home, so that your puppy cannot chew them. Make sure he has learned good chewing habits and is dependable before you give him the freedom of the house when he is left alone.

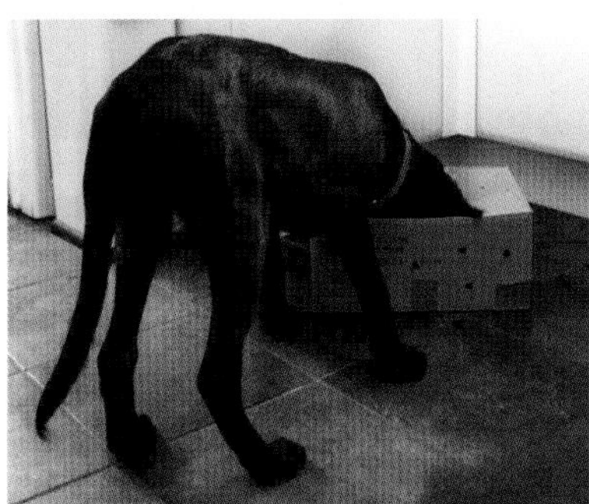

△ **Keeping busy**
Boxes with smaller boxes inside them filled with smelly treats and toys will use up some of your puppy's desire to investigate elsewhere.

When you are at home, keep your puppy entertained with different games and activities every hour. It is also a good idea to include him in jobs around the house—teach him to retrieve toys (pp.164–7) and ask him to help carry items for you. The more time he spends being busy with you, the less likely he is to get into trouble chewing things he should not, and, if he is working hard for your praise and attention, it will help to strengthen the bond between you.

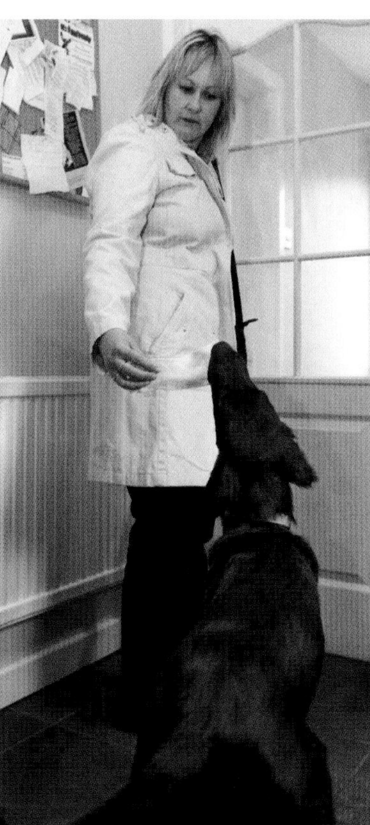

△ **Parting chew**
Giving your puppy a different chew each time you leave the house will keep him focused, and help prevent unwanted chewing.

Good manners

Dogs with nice manners are **easy to live with** and **pleasant to have around**. Like a child, your puppy is not born knowing right from wrong, but must **be taught how to behave**. As well as building a **respectful relationship** with your puppy, you will need to teach him about your **expectations** of him in **everyday life**. Follow the advice offered in this section, and your puppy will learn how to **behave well in all situations** around the home and outside it. He will not jump up, guard possessions, or snatch food. **Start these lessons early** and **plan ahead**, so that he is never rewarded for unacceptable behavior, and develops **good habits for life.**

SELF-CONTROL
To become well behaved, a puppy has to learn to control his impulses and realize that he needs to wait patiently for things he wants.

Building a good relationship

Getting the balance right between being a friend and being in control is not easy, but it is possible, especially if you set boundaries for your puppy early on and make it clear what you expect of him.

Love, trust, friendship

Puppies thrive with owners who are positive and encouraging, and who reward good behavior well. Building a relationship that is based on love, trust, and friendship will lead to a happy dog that works with you and is willing to please. Negativity and constant scolding make puppies nervous, withdrawn, and reluctant to try anything new.

The old-fashioned idea that you "must be boss" can rapidly slide into a master–slave relationship. This is crushing for a dog's spirit and a miserable way for him to live. Dogs have no desire to take over your world, and are usually happy to work with and for you if you are quick to praise their best efforts. This is especially true if you prove, over time, to be an effective leader, able to make good decisions that benefit all members of the pack.

▷ **Love and trust**
A puppy can only develop complete trust and an unwavering belief that he is safe if his owner is consistently kind, friendly, and positive.

▽ **Keep off, please**
It is important to set clear boundaries for behavior, and to make sure that your puppy learns what he is allowed to do—and will be rewarded for—and what he should not do.

Setting boundaries

Puppies, like children, do best with a parent figure who can take control when necessary to stop behavior getting out of hand, and who can keep everyone safe, calm, and ordered. If you set boundaries from the day your puppy arrives, and gently teach him what is acceptable and what is not (pp.116–7), he will get into good habits early on.

◁ **Patience is rewarded**
Rewarding good behavior every time, either with food or praise, will produce a puppy that works hard to do the right thing and knows what is necessary to please you.

“**Constant scolding** makes puppies **wary** of **trying anything new.**”

Throughout puppyhood, the best plan is to think ahead in order to prevent unwanted behavior, to stop anything that does occur that you don't like immediately, and to encourage, praise, and reward good behavior. Thinking ahead and preventing undesirable behavior will ensure that your puppy will never know how good it feels to be naughty. Stopping bad behavior as soon as it happens will mean that your puppy does not experience good feelings from unwanted behavior for too long. If you encourage good behavior, your puppy is more likely to opt for the behavior you want. This will give you the opportunity to praise and reward his good behavior, which, in turn, will result in it happening more often (pp.136–7).

When to say no

Once your puppy knows what is expected of him, and you are certain he knows how to behave well, you can make it clear to him that you will not accept alternative behavior—by saying no if he tries them. Immediately show him what you want him to do instead and praise him for doing it. In this way, you will make it really clear to him how he should behave. If you are resolute on keeping his behavior within boundaries, this will give him a sense of safety and stability, and he will feel more content than he would if he were allowed to do just as he pleased.

△ **Not for you**
Asking your puppy to restrain himself, and to wait for rewards when he wants something, will help him learn the self-control and calmness that are an important part of good manners.

▽ **Busy right now**
Your puppy needs to learn he cannot always have attention when he wants it, so practice time outs, where he is ignored for short periods.

Unwanted behavior

Teaching good manners involves showing your puppy what you want him to do and rewarding him for doing so, and never allowing him to learn how enjoyable bad behavior can be.

Self-rewarding behavior

It is important that your puppy does not learn to practice behavior that you do not like, and that you do not reward him if he does practice it. If you are careful to prevent your puppy from acquiring bad habits in his first year, and make sure he behaves well in all circumstances instead, he will not develop unwanted behavior later in life. Constant supervision and forward planning are essential if you are to achieve this. It is worth the effort though—you will be rewarded in the future with a dog that never behaves in an unacceptable way.

Jumping up

Puppies jump up to get closer to our faces. Make it a rule in the household that no one speaks to, looks at, or touches your puppy when his front legs are off the ground. This includes visitors, so use a leash to prevent your puppy jumping on them when they arrive. Simply wait until all his four feet are on the ground, and then crouch down to his level, praise gently, and give him lots of affection.

Counter surfing

Throughout your puppy's first year, get into the habit of putting all edible items away before leaving the kitchen, so that he does not learn to leap up to help himself to food from surfaces. In his first year,

△ **Ignore bad behavior**
If your puppy jumps up, fold your arms and do not look or speak to him. Keep still, so that he finds this behavior totally unrewarding and gets down again.

▷ **Reward good behavior**
As soon as all four feet are on the ground, get down to your puppy's level, and praise him warmly so that he knows he will be rewarded in future if he stays down.

if he jumps up and is not rewarded by finding food, he will stop thinking about doing so, and cease to check for things on the side.

Similarly, always think ahead when you place food on low tables, or if people are eating food from plates on their laps. Make sure your puppy is on a leash, so you can keep him at a distance and teach him not to snatch the food. Praise him well for not doing so, and give him a toy stuffed with food instead.

Barking

Puppies usually start alarm barking in earnest at about 7–8 months of age. It is important to discourage any excessive barking before this age so that your puppy learns to be quiet most of the time. If there is a reason for barking, such as a disturbance outside, get him into the habit of barking once to alert you, and then coming to you for food treats or for play.

Chasing

Chasing behavior needs to be diverted into chase games with toys as soon as possible, especially in puppies of breeds that were originally bred to chase, such as Border Collies. Teach them how to play with toys (pp.102–3), how to retrieve (pp.164–7), and how to do a chase recall (pp.170–1). For moving objects that you may have to pass every day, such as joggers and cyclists in the park or sheep in fields, habituate your puppy to their presence gradually (pp.82–3).

▷ **Clear counters**
Make sure that you put anything edible away once you have finished preparing food, so that your puppy does not learn to jump up and steal food from kitchen surfaces.

"**Your efforts** will be **rewarded** in future with a dog that **never shows unwanted behavior.**"

△ **Excited barking**
Stop unwelcome barking immediately by interrupting your puppy and expressing your disapproval, to prevent it becoming a bad habit.

▷ **Anticipate trouble**
If you see fast-moving people, animals, or wheels approaching, encourage your puppy to look to you for a fun game of chase instead.

Early learning
This puppy is rewarded when he investigates a box and finds a toy. If a puppy performs an action when young and is repeatedly rewarded for it, the action will develop into a life-long habit.

Food and **possession manners**

Dogs that will leave things when asked to, allow you to take food and possessions away from them, and take food gently when it is offered to them are nicer to have around than dogs that steal, guard, or snatch.

Teaching the "leave" is easy (see below). Once your puppy has learned this, you can teach him to leave other things that he values, rewarding him each time with something more special. It is also important to teach your puppy that hands come to give rather than to take, so that he does not learn to guard food or possessions (see facing page). He can then relax, knowing that you will not take things from him.

1 ▷

No way in

Show your puppy a treat, then wrap your hand around it, so the treat is in the center of your fist. Say "leave" and wait patiently. Do not repeat the cue or move your hand. Ignore anything he does.

2 ◁

Backing off

Wait patiently for your puppy to move his face away. Raise your hand slightly if he tries to paw you and ignore any chewing (put on an old, thick glove if he bites). Wait for the instant you feel his face move away from your hand.

3 ▷

Success!

Reward your puppy immediately. Once he understands what is required, ask him to leave toys or treats on low tables, using your hand as a cover if he goes to take them. Reward him well for holding back.

1 ▷

Tempt him

Wait until your puppy is a bit bored with his chew or other possession, and then approach with a tasty, smelly treat. Hold it out close to your puppy and wait for him to get up so that he can take the treat.

2 ◁

Fair exchange

Using the treat, lure your puppy away from his chew until you can pick it up with your other hand without him noticing. Once you have the chew safely in your hand, feed him the treat.

3 ▷

Give it back

Once your puppy has eaten the treat, give him back his chew. This way, he will learn that it is safe for you to approach him when he is eating or playing.

GOOD PRACTICE

Puppies that bite when you feed them are usually just inexperienced, and often catch you accidentally with their teeth as they try to take the food. Feed your puppy at first by placing the food on the flat of your hand, keeping your hand still and your thumb tucked in to give him the best chance to take the treat without error. When you are ready to go back to holding it between your thumb and finger, use larger pieces of food until he gets used to taking the treat gently.

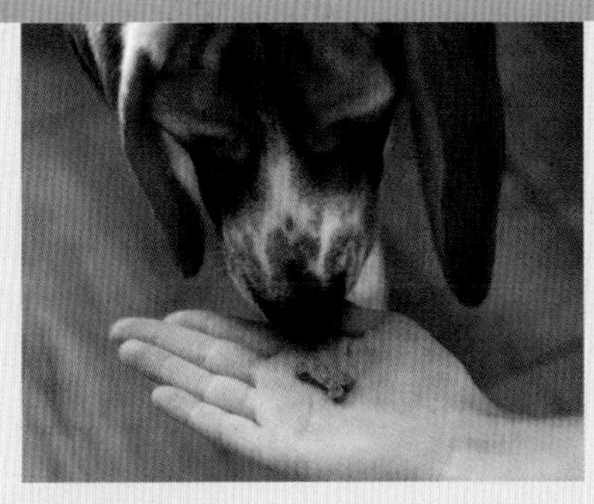

Nibble prevention

Offering food on the flat of your hand is a good way for young children to deliver treats without any risk of being nipped accidently.

Dealing with **frustration**

All puppies need to learn that they cannot have their own way all the time. They must find a way of dealing with the uncomfortable feelings that result from not getting what they want.

Difficult feelings

In a world where humans control most things, your puppy needs to learn that he cannot always have his own way. As you try to provide for his every need when he is young, it is tempting to respond to the smallest whimper or plea. Be careful—this approach can lead to your puppy believing that he can have anything he wants, which may result in problems later on.

When your puppy sees something he wants, he will try to get it. If he cannot, he will feel frustrated. This is not a comfortable feeling, as we all know—imagine a situation where you thought you were going to get something, but unexpectedly, it didn't arrive, or was taken by someone else. When these feelings first arise, your puppy will not know how to deal with them, and may react with behavior that helps him cope. If he really wants something and is very excited, he may bark, bite at whatever is around him, such as his leash, or throw himself around wildly. Just like toddlers screaming over candy they cannot have in a supermarket, your puppy's behavior may be extreme and embarrassing, even though it is

△ **Out of reach**
Throw an object, such as a toy, just out of reach, and use a leash to prevent your puppy from getting it. Start with a low value item to help him regain control of himself.

◁ **Calming down**
Do not speak to your puppy or touch him. Just wait patiently and watch him. He will go through a range of behaviors to try to manage the frustration he feels.

▷ **Release him**
Once your puppy has relaxed, let him go forward and have what he wanted. Through practicing this exercise, he will learn how to deal with frustration and will gain self-control.

a part of the natural learning process. For this reason, it is a good idea to teach your puppy how to cope with these feelings at home, rather than leaving it until such a situation arises in public.

Unless your puppy learns to deal with his frustration, the associated behaviors will get worse as he gets older. They are also more extreme in puppies that are genetically programmed to be more reactive. It is best to teach your puppy how to deal with frustration long before he reaches adolescence.

Coping strategy

Most puppies learn to deal with feelings of frustration naturally, as their owners slowly take control of them and their world as they mature. Asking your puppy to wait while you go through a door first, or to sit and wait before a toy is thrown, or to wait until you release him from the car to play, are all examples of situations where your puppy must put his desires aside to please you. If you practice this regularly as he grows, he will learn to deal with frustration gradually. Even so, there may still be certain situations—such as wanting to play with other dogs—where your puppy's feelings of excitement and frustration at not being allowed to join in overwhelm his normal self-control. For times like these, and for puppies that often feel frustrated, actively teaching them to remain calm will help.

Start your training with something that is of low value to your puppy, and slowly work up to things your puppy wants more. Work on problems at home first, then try again in real situations. The better your puppy learns to deal with feelings of frustration in everyday life, the better he will be able to cope when he is really excited.

◁ **Waiting politely**
Dogs with good manners are used to dealing with frustration. They will sit and wait politely, without fussing, until their owners allow them to do what they would prefer to do instead.

▽ **Frustration explosion**
Puppies need to learn early in life that they cannot have their own way, even in times of high excitement, and must wait until their owners allow them freedom.

Good behavior in the **car**

Having a dog that travels well in the car and is not sick, destructive, or dirty makes life much easier, and means that you can take him out with you wherever you are traveling to.

Successful journeys

Car travel can be a daunting experience for a small puppy, because of the noise of the car and the constant motion of the floor on which he is sitting. Since dogs do not have a seat to hold them securely in place, they have to keep their balance through every twist and turn in the road. It can take time for them to learn to balance, although it gets easier once they are large enough to see out of the car window. If your puppy is thrown around too much before he can see out, he may get hurt or frightened, and this can instill in him a lasting fear of car travel.

To avoid unnerving your puppy, consider using a travel crate, so he has something to lean against. Put a soft cushion or blanket inside to provide cushioning and support once the car starts moving.

Always drive as considerately as possible—this will give your puppy the chance to learn to balance and enjoy riding in the car. Allow plenty of time for your journey, so there is no need for you to rush, and take corners and bumps slowly

▷ **Up you go**
Lift your puppy into the car slowly and carefully to avoid alarming him at the start of the journey, and give him time to settle and feel comfortable before driving off.

◁ **Safely enclosed**
Using a properly secured travel crate will give your puppy something to lean against. Make sure it is large enough for him to turn around and lie down in.

△ **Make cars fun**
If your puppy is frightened, use games with toys and treats to encourage him to enjoy being near the car. Give him food and chews to get him used to being inside it.

and carefully so you do not unsettle him. Imagine that you are driving with a full glass of water in the car, and try to avoid spilling it. Start with very short journeys and gradually build up to longer ones. Try to take your puppy everywhere with you at first so he has several journeys a day. This will help him get used to travel more quickly.

When you bring your new puppy home from the breeder, take someone with you who can hold him on their lap—this way, he can avoid further upset when everything else around him is new.

Common problems

Some puppies really struggle with car journeys of any length. You may find that your puppy shows signs of distress even if you drive slowly in a straight line. Common signs of distress include car sickness or drooling, having diarrhea, barking, or chewing the car's interior.

In order to resolve these issues, you need to accept that it will take time and multiple journeys before your puppy feels safe in the car. Take things slowly, only going on very short journeys at first. Stop the car if your puppy begins to look unhappy, and allow him to get out and walk around to restore his equilibrium before you set off again. Gradually increase how far you go as he learns to cope better.

> “Use a **travel crate** with a soft **cushion or blanket** placed inside to transport your **puppy.**”

Your puppy needs to feel secure in the car, so settle him in a small area with a thick bed where he will not roll far if he loses his balance. If he has to accompany you on long journeys, accept that he may be sick or need to go to the bathroom. Take new bedding and waterproof layers with you, so that you can clean up several times if necessary.

As your puppy gets older, you may find that he becomes so excited about the prospect of a walk at the end of a car ride that he begins to bark frantically after getting into the car. To avoid this, do not drive off until he is quiet; stop and wait if he barks while you are driving (as long as it is safe to do so); and do not let him out of the car until he is completely silent. It also helps to do 10 minutes of obedience exercises when you get to your destination. He will gradually learn that it is advantageous for him to be quiet.

◁ **Car harness**
As an alternative to a crate, a well-fitting car harness will hold your puppy securely in place, and stop him from sliding off the seat if the car comes to a sudden halt.

▽ **Success**
If you take things slowly and allow time for your puppy to learn to travel well in the car, you will both arrive at your destination happy, relaxed, and ready to go.

Adolescence

When dogs go through adolescence, it can be a **challenging time** for **owners**, so **be prepared**. This section describes the **physical changes** that occur at **puberty**, and explains how these changes are likely to affect your dog's body and mind. If you are **mentally prepared** for the **shift in attitude** that your puppy will experience at this time, you will find it easier to **handle changes in his behavior**, and you will understand how to overcome any difficulties. Also remember that, no matter how bad things are, adolescence is a **temporary transition** into adulthood, and the **situation will improve** greatly **as your puppy matures.**

LEAVING HOME
Adolescence is a time when your maturing puppy will become much more interested in the outside world than in you and life at home.

Adolescent behavior

Behavioral changes during your dog's adolescence can be difficult to handle unless you are well prepared. Knowing how to deal with it and what to do will make life much easier for both of you.

Timing

Adolescence is the period between the start of puberty and the onset of maturity. In dogs, puberty begins at the age of 5–6 months—usually slightly earlier for smaller dogs and later for larger ones. The hormones that begin circulating in your dog's body at this age will change him from a puppy to a physically mature adult, and the process will take approximately 6 months (pp.130–1). By the time your dog is around 18 months to 2 years of age, he will have reached social maturity, which means that he has finished developing mentally as well.

Mind changes

Behavioral changes during this time can be dramatic and often have a negative impact on owners, as their puppy moves from having them as the center of his universe to becoming much more interested in his environment and others in it. Just like adolescence in humans, these changes can bring tough times for those experiencing them as well as for those around them. If owners know what to expect, and are prepared, they will cope better. Before puberty begins, a puppy is

◁ **Young and vulnerable**
Before puberty, your puppy is dependent on you for food and protection. He will work hard to please you and be very loving.

△ **Outside interests**
During adolescence, your puppy may seem to change dramatically—no longer interested in the family, in pleasing you, or in responding to cues. He will instead be focused only on finding out about the outside world.

△ **High-value treats**
Keep working on your puppy's exercises, but make sure you have high-value rewards to give him a good incentive. Do not expect him to work just for praise and attention.

◁ **Secure attachment**
While your puppy is more interested in the outside world than you, use a long line to prevent him from running off and getting into trouble. Be careful not to get tangled in it.

young and vulnerable, and unable to survive by itself. As puberty strikes, the puppy begins to be more independent and more interested in the outside world.

How to manage

It is important to keep control of your puppy during adolescence. Control the resources he needs, such as food and access to the outdoors, so that he has to pay attention to you, and work for what he wants. Build on your relationship too, but do not be offended if your affection is not always reciprocated, especially if your puppy's mind is elsewhere. Keep trying, and make interactions fun and good-natured. Invite your puppy to play. He may not be interested, especially when he is outside, but try to engage him and keep games short. Make sure your training sessions are fun and you do not expect too much. If you have done lots of training before this point, it will be easier for your puppy to get through the adolescent stage. Remember that eventually adolescence comes to an end, and it is just a phase that he has to go through in order to grow up.

"During **puberty,** your **puppy** will become **more interested** in the **outside world.**"

▷ **Stolen moments**
During adolescence, your puppy still needs you, but he will want to be close to you less often. Eventually, as he matures, he will become interested in you once again.

Changing bodies

The onset of puberty brings considerable changes to puppies' bodies as they become ready for reproduction. Owners need to make decisions about neutering and breeding at this stage.

Timing

Puberty for dogs begins at the age of 5–6 months, when the hormones that prepare their bodies for reproduction begin circulating. They bring about all the physical changes that will occur over the next 6 months. Dogs' bodies go through a considerable upheaval at this time, as do their minds.

Female dogs first come into season between 6–12 months of age, and are then attractive to unneutered males for around 3 weeks—although mating usually happens around the 10th day. After this, seasons occur at roughly 6-month intervals, unless a female is neutered. Males become sexually mature at about 6 months of age. If they are left unneutered, they develop other characteristics, such as thickened skin on the neck and bulkier muscles, in their first year.

Neutering

The process of neutering takes away a dog's reproductive organs, which produce the hormones that cause the biggest changes to a dog's body and mind.

In females, the uterus and ovaries are removed under anesthetic. This operation is usually done several

△ **Lapse in housebreaking**
At puberty, a temporary loss of housebreaking may occur, particularly in females. Males begin to cock one leg as hormones start circulating.

▽ **Planned litters**
Only breed from dogs that have no behavioral problems and excellent temperaments, and make sure you can find loving homes for the puppies.

△ **No competition**
Neutered male dogs are less likely to be competitive with unneutered males and will not run off to find females in season.

▷ **Neutering decisions**
If you are not planning to breed from your dog, it is advisable to consider neutering. Research the positive and negative aspects, then make a decision early, in consultation with your vet.

months after a female dog's first season, when her reproductive organs are in a resting state. There are many health benefits to neutering a female—it eliminates the risk of an infected uterus later in life, and reduces the risk of mammary tumors. In addition, she cannot get pregnant or come into season every 6 months, so it removes the necessity to supervise her carefully during this time to avoid her getting close to males.

In males, the testes are removed under anesthetic, usually after puberty, at about 7 months of age. This stops the high levels of testosterone they produce from circulating around the body, and has a beneficial, calming effect.

Breeding

Before you breed from your dog, pay a visit to your local animal shelter housing unwanted dogs. Many are put to sleep each day, because there are always too many dogs for the number of homes available. By breeding from your dog, you will be adding to their number. What if you cannot find homes for the puppies? Are you able to keep those you do not sell, and are you in a position to take back any puppies that "do not work out" with their new owners?

"If you **decide** to **breed** from your dog, get all the **health tests done beforehand.**"

If you decide to go ahead, first ensure your dog has been tested for any inherited diseases. Carefully research what tests are needed, and how to interpret the results. Also consider the temperament of the mother and the father, as well as their parents and grandparents.

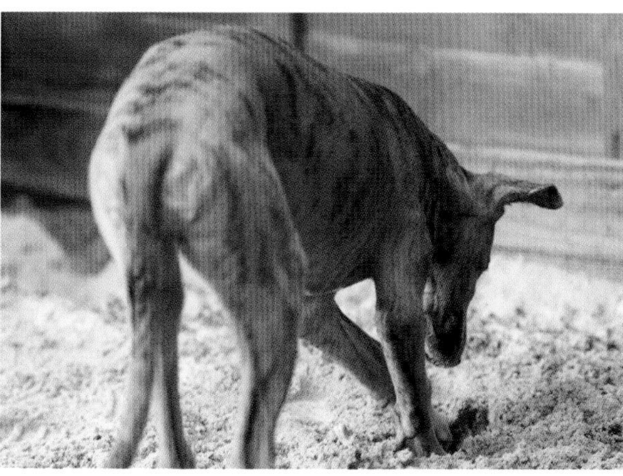

▷ **Escape bid**
A female dog will try to get out to search for a mate around the 10th day of her season, when she is ovulating. Watch your female dog carefully during this time.

Training

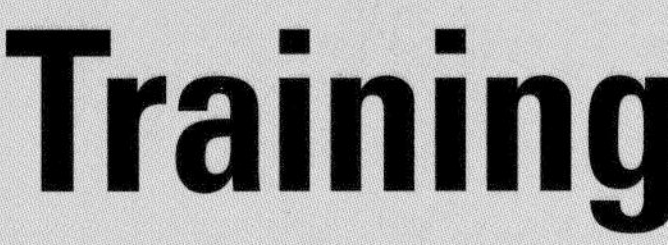

How puppies learn

Finding out how puppies learn can save you and your puppy a lot of time and frustration. If you understand how the learning process works, you will be a **more successful trainer**. This section explains how puppies **figure out** what we need them to do, what they **find rewarding**, how to **time your rewards** accurately, and how to get **responses** to **voice cues** and **hand signals**. With this knowledge, your training will be **fast** and **effective**. You will be able to **communicate more successfully** with your puppy, and **the relationship** you have with him will be **stronger**.

EFFECTIVE LEARNING Learning about luring, timing, hand signals, and rewards will give you a firm foundation for teaching your puppy any exercise or trick.

Trial, error, and success

Puppies learn in the same way children do: by a process of trial, error, and success. As owners, we need to arrange things so that puppies show correct behaviors, which we can then reward and put on cue (pp.142–3).

Learning

Both humans and animals learn by trying an action and finding it rewarding, unrewarding, or unpleasant. If an action is rewarded, they are likely to do it again. If it goes unrewarded, they may do it again but not often. If they found it unpleasant, they will cease to do it.

For example, if your puppy puts his head in an open garbage can and finds food or a tissue to play with, he is likely to raid them from that moment on, particularly if his behavior is reinforced by subsequent finds. If, in contrast, he finds it is empty, even after several investigations, he is likely to give up checking, and once he is mature, he will not even think to look. Finally, if your puppy looks in a garbage can and his head gets stuck, it may scare him so much that he will not go near one again. A sensitive puppy may avoid areas around it, or even the room that it's in, for a while afterward. In this way, puppies learn from experience.

▷ **Tasty treasure**
Finding food inside the garbage can will encourage this puppy to look again later. If he often discovers food rewards, turning it over for its contents will become an established habit.

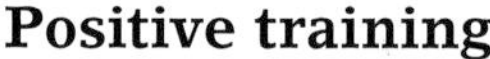

Positive training

You can make use of a puppy's ability to learn from his actions by rewarding your puppy whenever he does something you approve of. To train your puppy, all you need to do is to encourage him to perform the action you require and reward him for doing so (see below).

△ **Encourage the action: sit**
Hold the reward high—in this case, your puppy's food. If he has to look up and back for a long time, it is easier for him to sit than stand.

△ **Reward the action**
As soon as your puppy sits, reward him. This will encourage him to do what you want the next time he is in the same place and situation.

△ **Put it on cue: hand signal**
Eventually, after lots of repetition, your puppy will respond to a cue, even though the reward is out of sight and he has to work on trust.

△ **Family activity**
Encouraging children to join in training will mean that everyone in the family can communicate with the puppy in the same way, and learn to encourage appropriate behavior and good manners.

This method is not as easy as it sounds, because you cannot use words to tell a puppy what you want him to do, or to let him know when he has done the right thing. To overcome this communication problem, we need to rely on clever methods to get a puppy to do what we want, timing rewards accurately so that he knows he has done well.

Actions can be encouraged in many ways. The most effective of these is luring, where a small piece of food is used to tempt the puppy slowly into the position you require. If you want your puppy to sit, for example, you need to raise the treat above his head, so he naturally has to sit down to get at it (pp.148–9). Alternatively, showing your puppy that you have something he wants and then moving away works for exercises such as coming when called (pp.150–1) or walking on a loose leash (pp.158–61).

Timing is critical. To let your puppy know he has done the right thing, reward him as soon as he does the action (pp.140–1). The better your timing, the faster he will learn. Once your puppy is repeatedly performing the right action, you can begin to teach him to do it in response to a hand signal or voice cue (pp.142–3). You can also progress to practicing in new places, with distractions (pp.144–5).

"**Luring** is an **effective way** of **encouraging actions**. A small **piece of food** is used to **tempt the puppy** into the **right position.**"

Rewards

Rewards are an important part of positive training. They motivate your puppy to behave in the way you want them to. Once delivered, they are an obvious signal that he has done the right thing.

What to use

A reward can be anything that your puppy wants at that moment in his life. He may be hungry and want food, or playful and want a game, or in need of affection. He may want to investigate an item you've picked up, or he may want to go out on a walk. Almost anything can be used—provided he wants it at that point in time. Owners usually use food when training puppies, since puppies are often hungry.

△ **Bite-sized**
Limit the size of food rewards. Offer pieces that are equal to a large pea for a medium-sized puppy, and adjust the treat size slightly for bigger or smaller puppies.

Praise

Puppies will work for your praise and approval alone, since both are important to them. Even so, because they can get approval from you for free most of the time, they will not usually work very hard to earn it. It is a good idea to use praise in addition to food when teaching your puppy new exercises. Praise him warmly and genuinely when he responds to your requests, and he will work harder to please you next time.

Using food

For food to be successful as a training tool, it must be tasty and appealing to a puppy. The pieces also need to be the right size, and the value of the food to him must be equal to the work he is expected to do for it. Each piece should be about the size of a large pea. If you feed big pieces, your puppy will get full too quickly. If your treats are too small, he may not bother to work for them.

Different foods have different values to your puppy. Experiment to find out which treats he likes best, and order them for use in a hierarchy of value. Reserve his favorite foods for difficult tasks, such as learning new exercises, or offer them at times when you ask him to do one thing and he would rather do something else—such as coming back from playing with another dog.

◁ **Gentle praise**
Try not to handle your puppy roughly when praising him. Patting his head may unsettle, distract, or confuse him. Use gentle touches on the chest instead.

Tasty, smelly treats

Puppies work best for food that is smelly and soft, with a high meat content. Dry biscuits, by comparison, are rarely worth working hard for, unless your puppy has a high motivation for food. Try lots of different foods to find his favorite.

Hot dog pieces

Cheese cubes

Cooked chicken

Cooked sausage

Bite-sized treats

Moist treats

Meaty strips

Use medium-value food rewards for exercises your puppy has already learned and is practicing, and give him low-value foods in return for good manners, such as sitting down and waiting while a door is opened. His favorite food one week will not necessarily be the same the next week, so keep track of changes to the hierarchy.

To work well for food, your puppy needs to be a little hungry, but not ravenous. If he is very hungry, he will be too focused on food, and will find it difficult to think about what he has to do to earn it. If your puppy is too hungry to concentrate, feed him a small meal and give him time to digest it before trying again.

▷ **Toy rewards**
Toys should only be used once your puppy has learned to enjoy playing with them. Until it is obvious that he has developed a real enthusiasm for toys, continue using food as a reward during training.

▽ **Latent learning**
Puppies seem to learn while they rest—when they resume training after a nap, they are more likely to get a task right the first time. No one knows why this is the case, but if you let your puppy rest often, he will learn more rapidly.

"**Different foods** have different **values** to your puppy. **Find out** which **treats** he **likes best.**"

Successful timing

Good timing is important and helps your puppy learn quickly. A reward given at the appropriate time, just as the action happens, lets him know he has done the right thing, so he will be more likely to repeat it.

Good timing

Delivering a treat or other reward to your puppy the instant he does the right thing helps him learn to offer that behavior again in the future. By giving rewards, you are letting your puppy know that he is correct. The more immediate the delivery of the reward, the faster he will learn.

Staged rewards

If your puppy is struggling to understand a more difficult task, such as learning to lie down by being lured from a sitting position (pp.152–3), it may help to reward smaller movements in the right direction. This is called shaping, and will encourage him to keep trying—puppies rapidly give up if they try and are not successful the first time. Reward your puppy simply for looking down at first, then for moving a little closer to the ground, then closer still. He will slowly realize that you are asking him to lie down and, eventually, he will sink to his elbows. It is all about communicating by delivering rewards. To your puppy, a reward proves that an action was worthwhile, so he will want to repeat it. Later on, putting the same action on cue (pp.142–3) will be straightforward, because

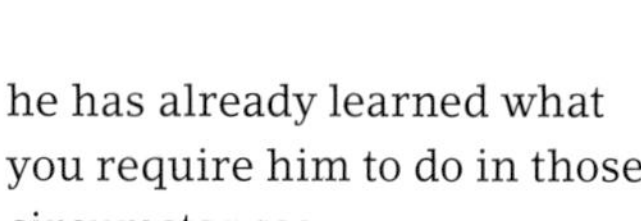
he has already learned what you require him to do in those circumstances.

▷ Luring
Where a dog's nose goes, the body follows. Luring your puppy is a useful way of getting him to adopt positions, so that you can put these actions on cue.

◁ Shaping
This owner wants her puppy to look for a toy that is hidden in the box (pp.180–1). Each time he moves a step closer, he is given a treat. Rewarding small efforts motivates your puppy.

▽ Targeting
Over several sessions, dogs can be taught to touch a target—here, a hand. By moving the target, you can get your puppy to do things he would not naturally do, such as close doors.

Success signal

As well as delivering the treat instantly, you can give your puppy a verbal signal that you are pleased. Something like "Yes!" is fine, provided this is not something you say to him at any other time. If you repeatedly give this signal when he does the right thing, he will begin to associate it with success.

Once your puppy has learned the cue for an action, and understands what he is expected to do, you can use this signal alone to let him know he was right—and you don't always have to offer him a reward. This is the principle behind clicker training, but a single word works just as well if you are consistent.

The advantage of creating a verbal signal is that you always have it with you. Make sure that

"The **advantage** of a **verbal signal** is that you **always** have it **with you**. Make sure the **word** you use **remains constant.**"

△ **Perfect timing**
In this picture, the puppy was rewarded as soon as his bottom hit the ground. The result? He will be much more likely to sit when he is asked next time.

▷ **Too late**
The treat has been lost in the bottom of the pocket, seconds have elapsed, and the puppy is now thinking about something other than sitting down.

the word you choose to use remains constant, delivering it with the same excitement and tone each time so that your puppy can recognize it easily. With practice, you will be able to use your signal as a bridge between an action and the ensuing reward, so that timing becomes less critical and you do not always have to reward an action your puppy is really familiar with immediately. Your success signal lets him know that he did the right thing in the right circumstance. In this way, even if your puppy isn't rewarded with food every time, he will still feel successful, and rewards can then be given randomly (p.145).

◁ **Social aspects**
Puppies learn by getting caught up in the excitement of a situation—not by copying. If one dog jumps up and barks, another may do the same, as a natural response to the excitement.

Cues and **signals**

Putting actions and behavior on cue will let your puppy know exactly what to do whenever that cue is given. Hand signals are easier for puppies to learn than vocal commands.

On cue

Once your puppy knows the action you want him to do (pp.136–7), you can begin to put it on cue. To do this, your puppy has to learn to associate something you do—the cue, which will be either a hand signal or a word—with the action itself. This is difficult when you cannot tell him what you mean.

To help your puppy understand what a cue means, get him to practice the desired movement—for example, sitting—a few times. Your sequence should be: lure (p.137)—action (puppy sits)—reward and praise. Once your puppy performs the action every time you ask for it, your sequence becomes: cue—lure—action—reward and praise.

Practice the new sequence many times over several sessions until it becomes automatic for both of you. To make it as straightforward as possible for your puppy, be clear with your cues and always give them just before the action begins.

Eventually, change the sequence to: cue—pause—lure—action—reward and praise. The pause of just a few seconds will give your puppy time to think. During this time, he will try to figure out what he has to do. Let him think without making any noise. If he has not responded after a few seconds, use the lure to help him out. If he does

◁ **Clear signal**
Make your movements very exaggerated at first, so that your puppy can clearly see that this hand signal is different from another.

▽ **Immediate reward**
Remember to give the reward immediately after the action—in this case, lying down. As your puppy learns, you can slowly make your signals less and less exaggerated.

the action without the lure, reward him well and give him lots of praise. Then repeat the sequence one more time and end the session. After lots of practice, you will be able to take the lure out of the sequence entirely.

The learning curve

Don't be surprised if your puppy's learning seems to go backward at times before going forward again, even if he appears to have forgotten everything. This is perfectly normal, so just be patient and show him what to do again. Remember that learning can be very tiring for a young dog, so make sure you give him plenty of time to rest in between sessions.

Hand signals or words?

Puppies learn body movements or hand signals much more readily than spoken commands because of the way their brains function (pp.66–7). When you begin to teach a new exercise, use hand signals as your cues rather than words.

Once your puppy is responding to your hand signal every time, and no longer needs the lure, move on to adding a command word ahead of the hand signal. Speak quietly—there is no need to shout. The sequence now becomes: verbal cue—hand signal—action—reward and praise. Eventually, you can phase out the hand signal, but do so only once he is responding reliably to the verbal cue.

> "Give **verbal cues quietly**—there is **no need** to **raise** your **voice.**"

Hand signals

The key to success with cues is repetition. The more times your dog sees a clear, obvious hand signal before being lured into position, the quicker he will respond. Practice hand signals prior to training to avoid confusing your dog.

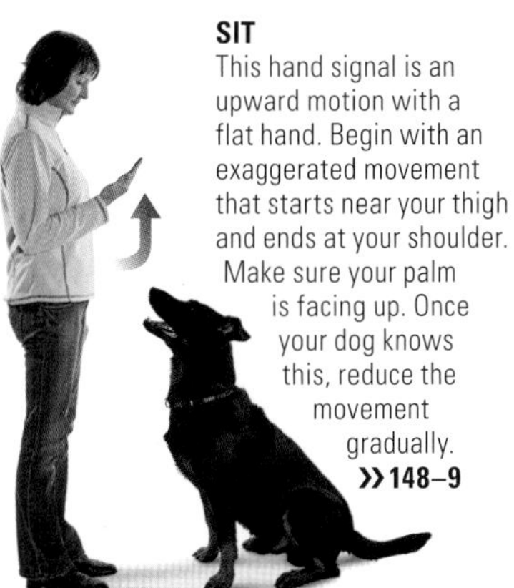

SIT
This hand signal is an upward motion with a flat hand. Begin with an exaggerated movement that starts near your thigh and ends at your shoulder. Make sure your palm is facing up. Once your dog knows this, reduce the movement gradually.
»148–9

COME
This signal consists of a movement of the arms held alongside the body and then brought out from the body to the position shown here. When you first begin training using this exercise, you will be crouching, so the movement starts with the hands together, then the arms are raised outward to either side.
»150–1

WAIT
To give this signal, hold your hand flat, palm down, then bring it down slowly toward your dog's face and hold it stationary. Try to position your hand so that your dog can still see your face; otherwise, he may move in order to try to see around it.
»154–5

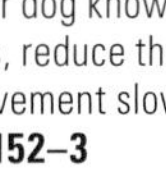

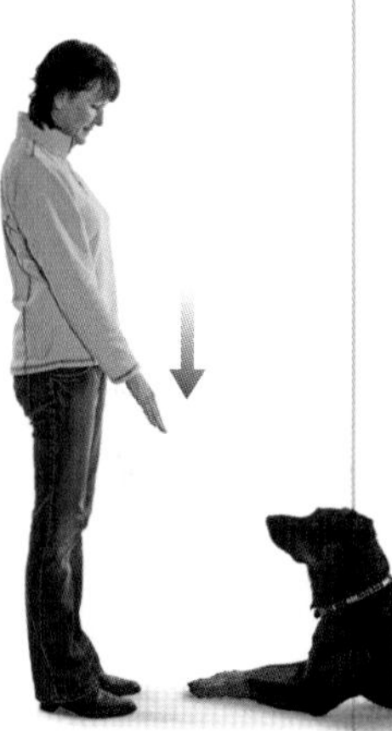

DOWN
This hand signal consists of a downward motion with a flat hand. Begin with an exaggerated movement that starts near your shoulder and ends at the thigh. The palm should be facing down. Once your dog knows this, reduce the movement slowly.
»152–3

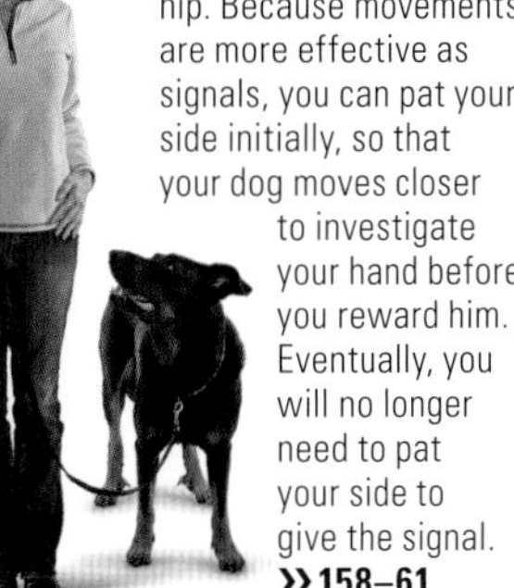

HEEL
Hold your hand on your hip. Because movements are more effective as signals, you can pat your side initially, so that your dog moves closer to investigate your hand before you reward him. Eventually, you will no longer need to pat your side to give the signal.
»158–61

STAND
For the "stand" signal, hold a flat hand in front of your dog's nose, then draw it away. The palm of your hand should be facing your dog's nose. Reduce the signal gradually once he knows what you are asking him to do.
»156–7

Associations and **distractions**

For cues and signals to work anywhere, we need to teach our puppies to respond to them in many different places and situations, with lots of interesting things going on in the background.

Associations

When you start training your puppy, make sure you begin each session in the same place, with him in the same position in relation to you. When puppies learn, they learn the whole set of associations surrounding an event, rather than just the cue and action that you want them to learn. Being consistent will help your puppy—if you change the associations too quickly, he will get confused. For example, if you teach your puppy to sit in the living room while you are sitting down, he will not understand what to do if you then ask him to sit outside on the sidewalk when you are standing up. He is not being disobedient—he is simply unable to link the cue to the action in the new context.

To overcome this confusion, you will need to teach your puppy the same cue in lots of different places, varying your position in relation to him. Practice in one place for several sessions, so that he really understands what to do before you move on to somewhere new. Then repeat your training in many different circumstances, and your puppy will eventually connect the cue with the action every time, regardless of where he is or whether you are sitting or standing.

Learning with distractions

Once your puppy has learned that certain cues mean certain actions, real-life training can begin. Choose an environment that is quiet and with few distractions. You can start at home, teaching your puppy exercises while someone plays with his favorite toy in the background. If he is too distracted to pay

△ **Early learning**
Begin teaching your puppy a new exercise in a place where there are no distractions, such as your living room, so that he can concentrate. Do your training in lots of short sessions over a period of several days or weeks.

▷ **Puzzled**
Don't expect your puppy to understand your cue and respond correctly when he is somewhere different, even though he knows the cue well and will respond immediately when back in a familiar place.

△ **Start again**
Go back to basics each time you are somewhere new, asking for the action and then luring your puppy into position, until he understands what you want him to do.

"Puppies learn the associations around an event, rather than just the cue and action you teach."

attention to you, move away or reduce the toy play until he can focus. Make sure you use high value rewards (pp.138–9) and reward him well for prolonged periods of concentration, letting him go and investigate the toy.

Slowly work up to training your puppy in really distracting situations—for example, in the park, with children playing around him. Also practice in places where there are other things that your puppy would prefer to do, such as play with other dogs. If he is struggling to focus, start again from basics until you get a response that you can reward.

▷ **Well trained**
Build up to practicing in situations that your puppy finds exciting—for example, while children, cyclists, or joggers move past quickly, or while other dogs play in the distance.

△ **Back to basics**
Your heelwork (pp.160–3) may fall apart in the presence of another dog, because the situation is too stimulating for your puppy to focus. Be patient and revert to basic training, using a lure to get your puppy to concentrate.

Random rewards

Once your puppy will reliably respond to all the cues you give him, you can begin to reduce the number of rewards he gets. Do this gradually, sometimes giving him praise alone for doing the right thing. To make up for times when he only gets praise, and to mark really good performances, randomly give him "jackpots." A jackpot should be made up of many of his favorite things, including high-value treats and games with toys. If your puppy "wins" a jackpot, celebrate with him, making it a special occasion.

▷ **Top prize**
Keep jackpots—an assortment of his favorite treats and games—for really good performances. Your puppy will begin to gamble on the outcome of his response, putting in more effort each time to try to win the big prize.

The basics

Teaching your puppy the basic exercises in this section will mean he grows up to be **easy to live with**, and **responsive** to your **words and gestures**. You will be able to position him easily, **call him back**, ask him to **stay**, retrieve objects, or **walk next to you**. Building on the basics, you can then **teach your puppy exercises that could save his life during an emergency**, such as a recall from a chase or sit at a distance. **Positive training** will build a **strong bond** between you and your puppy and enhance your relationship. And **a well-trained puppy is much more likely to be welcomed** by people in any situation than an unruly one.

RESPONSIVE PUPPY
Teaching your puppy to respond to cues in return for rewards will make life with him both easier and more enjoyable.

Sit

The sit position is useful for keeping your puppy still and temporarily in one place. It allows you to gain control quickly at times of excitement. Puppies learn to sit easily because their owners often ask them to do it.

Teach your puppy to sit using the method below, so that he learns to follow the lure (stages 1 and 2), then teach him to respond to a cue (stage 3). Once he sits promptly and reliably at home, teach him the exercise from the beginning in different places. Teach him to sit in various positions in relation to you, too—for example, beside you rather than in front of you, or with you sitting down.

1. ◁

Move the treat up and back

Place a treat close to your puppy's nose and move it slowly up and back so that he has to tilt his head back to reach it. Let him lick and chew at the treat to keep him interested.

"Once **your puppy** knows how **to sit, teach** him to do it in **different places.**"

2. ▷

Bottom down

As your puppy's head goes over and back, his bottom should sink slowly toward the ground since this will be more comfortable for him. As soon as his bottom touches the ground, feed him the treat and praise him. Repeat stages 1 and 2 over several sessions, so that he easily follows the lure of a treat into a sitting position before you introduce a hand signal.

3

Introduce a cue

Give your puppy a clear hand signal (p.143), wait a moment, then lure him into position with a treat. After enough repetitions, he will learn to anticipate by sitting on cue before you lure him with a treat. Reward him generously.

4

Roadside practice

Give your puppy plenty of practice at responding on cue in different places, with distractions around him, and in various positions in relation to you. Then he will be easily able to respond to the "sit" cue when it matters—at the curb.

GOOD PRACTICE

If and when you introduce a voice command, be careful not to ask your puppy to "sit down," since this gives him two conflicting cues—"sit" and "down."

Don't press on your puppy's bottom to put him into a sit, because this can damage developing joints and bones.

Once your puppy knows the cue to sit, try training him when he is excited and would rather do something else. Begin when he is only slightly excited.

Useful skill
If you train your dog to sit at times of high excitement, you can keep him with you even when you greet visitors.

Treat too high
Holding the treat too high makes your puppy jump up rather than sit down. Be sure to hold it at nose level first, before taking it up and back.

Come when **called**

Teaching your puppy to come back to you when called allows you to let him off the leash safely in public areas. It also enables you to give him more exercise and freedom.

First train your puppy how to come when called at home. Once he reliably returns, even when you are out of sight, teach him again in different places. Before he reaches puberty he is much more likely to come when you call, so make the most of this early opportunity by taking him to safe places to practice. In open areas without boundaries, use a long leash to let him loose, but keep him safe.

1. △

Show the treat
Ask a friend to hold your puppy's collar. Place a tempting treat near your puppy's nose while your friend prevents him from moving forward. Walk backward for a short distance of about 6ft (2m) and crouch down so that you are at your puppy's level.

2. ▷

Call him
Make sure your puppy is paying attention and is eager to get to you before you call. Ask your friend to release him as soon as you start calling, and open your arms wide to encourage him to come to you.

"Before **puberty, your puppy** is most **likely** to **come** when **called,** since he feels too **vulnerable** to leave you."

New horizons
Once your puppy has learned to come, try calling him without a friend there to restrain him, and also when you are out of sight. Call him to you in different places. Take him to a safe, open area far away from traffic and practice there, rewarding him with praise and high value treats when he responds.

3 △ ▷

Encourage and reward
As your puppy comes to you, keep your arms wide open until the last moment, softly encouraging him with your voice. As he nears you, lure him in with the treat. Hold his collar (but don't reach out for it) with the other hand. Reward him with praise and the treat.

GOOD PRACTICE

To make sure your puppy is reliable about responding, practice in many places, and gradually increase distractions. Only call him when you think you will be successful. Give him his favorite reward when you ask for something difficult, such as abandoning play with other dogs.

If your puppy is shy, help to speed up his return by turning sideways and looking away so that he doesn't feel pressured.

Later, you can use games as a reward, but keep to edible treats until your puppy has learned how to play with you.

The best time to let your puppy off the leash is when he is still young and feels vulnerable enough not to leave you. Gradually build his ability and desire to come back to you, even in exciting circumstances, until he responds reliably every time. If you cannot let him off safely, use a long leash to give him freedom while he learns—but be careful not to tangle yourself or others in it.

Ignoring distractions
Practice until your puppy will come to you as soon as you call, whatever else is happening—even if it is something really exciting, like other dogs playing close by.

Down

The down position is useful for keeping your puppy still and encouraging him to settle in an exciting situation. It also teaches him self-control, since he has to learn to remain down even when he wants to get up.

Start by luring your puppy into the down position, following stages 1–3, shown here. Be patient, since it can take him a while to learn this. Once he is going down easily, introduce a hand signal (p.143).

Then progress to teaching your puppy to lie down in different places and with distractions around him. Continue to practice until your puppy can be relied upon to lie down on cue in any situation.

1. ◁

Lure his head down
Ask your puppy to sit (pp.148–9). Lure his head slowly downward with a tasty treat close to his nose. Keep his attention by letting him lick and chew tiny pieces off the treat. Hold the treat firmly, so that he cannot finish it in one gulp.

"Be **patient** when **teaching** the **down position.**"

2. ▷

Draw his body down
Direct your puppy slowly downward by moving the treat straight down. Keep him focused by letting him lick and chew at small pieces of the treat. If he stands up, put him back into the sit position before moving him down again.

3 ▽

Elbows to the ground

Watch your puppy's elbows. As soon as both are on the ground, feed him the rest of the treat immediately and praise him warmly. The down position may take a long time to achieve at first, but the next time, it will be quicker.

4 ▷

Hand signal

After several sessions, when your puppy is reliably going straight down as you lure him, introduce a cue. Get his attention, give a clear hand signal, and then, after a short pause, lure him into the down position as before.

GOOD PRACTICE

Once your puppy is reliably responding to the "down" cue, train him to settle. At first, attach a leash to stop him from wandering, and place him on a soft bed next to you. Ask him to settle by giving him the cue to lie down, then reward him with a chew when he does so. Sit back to read or watch television and leave him to relax. If he gets up, ask him to lie down again, and reward him with plenty of praise when he does so. Once he will reliably settle with you at home, teach him to respond in other situations, such as when you have visitors.

Settle down
Practice with friends to make sure your puppy can settle when visitors arrive, or when you take him to other people's houses.

Wait

Teaching your puppy to wait is useful for keeping him still when you need to move away, such as when opening the door to visitors.

Begin teaching your puppy to wait when he is tired, to make it easier for him to stay still. Practice the wait with you staying still over several sessions until you can rely on him to remain seated. This builds a good foundation before you begin to ask him to wait while you move around him.

1 ▷

Sitting for a second
Your puppy needs to have learned to sit on cue (pp. 148–9) before you begin. In a quiet, non-distracting place, ask your puppy to sit. Give the "wait" hand signal (p. 143) and keep still for just one second.

"Wait!"

"Good boy!"

2 △

Reward him
Deliver the reward to your puppy so that he does not have to move. Praise him and repeat, increasing the time between cue and reward. If he moves, reposition and try again with a shorter wait.

GOOD PRACTICE

Once your puppy understands the hand signal to wait and stays put wherever you happen to be in the room, take him out to teach him to wait in other places, such as the yard or the park. Start in quiet areas and then gradually build up the level of distraction he is exposed to.

When your puppy can work well in distracting circumstances, begin to ask him to wait in situations where he would rather move, such as when both of you are going through a doorway together. This will be challenging, so keep things calm at first with slow movements. Reward him well. Once he can manage to let you go through a doorway first, ask him to wait in more and more exciting circumstances. Eventually, he will learn to wait reliably even during times of high excitement—for example, when visitors arrive at the house. Waiting while you answer the door is one of the most useful applications of this exercise.

Patience
This puppy patiently waits for release and reward even though he may want to go outside or rush to greet his owner.

3 ▽

Move away

After several sessions, when your puppy is able to wait for up to two minutes on cue, slowly begin to move away by taking a step back. Move forward and reward your puppy in position. Over time, gradually move farther away.

4 △

Move around him

Once your puppy is comfortable with you moving away from him, begin to move to the side, just one step at first, before returning with the reward. When you move behind him, he may get up. Reposition and try again slowly.

"Once **your puppy understands** the cue **to wait, take him out** to learn in a **park.**"

Stand

Learning to stand on cue is essential if you intend to show your puppy when he is older. It is also easier to groom and bathe your puppy when he is standing up, and for the vet to check him in this position.

If you are considering showing your puppy in the future, teach him to stand while he is still young. Practice the standing position a little more than the sitting position (pp.148–9), and your puppy will use the stand as his default position when he wants to earn a treat. Even if you do not intend to go to dog shows, "stand" is a useful cue to get him up from a sitting position when you need to examine him.

1.

Start in sit

Ask your puppy to sit. Put a treat near his nose and let him lick and chew at it. Move the treat slowly away from your puppy, keeping it parallel to the ground, so that he follows it with his nose horizontal.

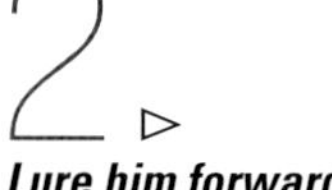

Lure him forward

Continue to lure your puppy forward until his back legs begin to lift his bottom. Slow the movement of the treat at this point so that he lifts his back end but does not move his front feet. Feed him the treat and praise him.

"**Work on** your puppy's ability to understand the cue by **training in places with distractions.**"

3 ▽

Introduce the hand signal

Repeat stages 1 and 2 over several sessions, with you standing rather than kneeling, until your puppy reliably follows the lure of the treat into a standing position. Then bring in your cue, giving a clear hand signal (p.143) before luring him up with a treat.

4 △

New set of associations

Once your puppy is responding to your hand signal, start again from stage 1, using a lure, but this time with you sitting on a chair. When he understands, try again in different places and with distractions.

GOOD PRACTICE

Start training somewhere quiet, without distractions, and in a situation where there is no reason for your puppy to want to sit. Gradually work on his ability to understand the cue by training in different places with distractions going on around him. Later, once your puppy is reliable and understands what to do, you can use the cue in places where he may be a little uncertain about standing up. Gently help him to realize that no harm will come to him if he does so.

Unless you own a show dog, you may decide that you do not need to teach this exercise. But it can be useful in other circumstances, such as trips to the vet's or grooming sessions.

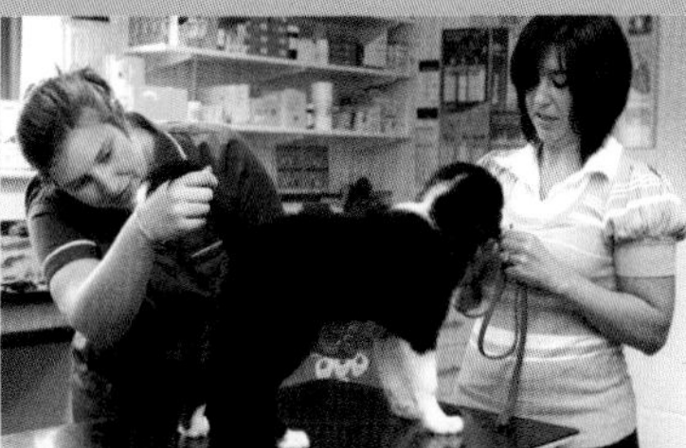

Veterinary check-up
A puppy that will stand on cue, even in a stressful situation when he would rather sit, is easier for a vet to examine.

Walking on a **loose leash 1**

A puppy that has learned how to walk on the leash without pulling and actively attempts to keep the leash loose will grow into an adult dog that is easy to exercise and a pleasure to take out.

Teaching your puppy to walk well on the leash is not easy and needs patience. Be prepared for it to take some time for both of you to master the skills required. To begin, teach your puppy that he will be rewarded if he walks on one side of you, fairly close to your leg. Once this basic principle is in place, you can teach him to keep the leash loose at all times when out for a walk (pp.160–1).

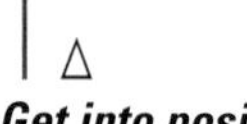

1 △

Get into position
Put the handle of the leash in your right hand. With a tasty treat in your left hand, lure your puppy around in a big arc behind you until he is standing beside your leg. Feed him the treat.

2 ▷

Gain his attention
Show your puppy you have another treat by briefly putting it near his nose. It does not matter whether he is sitting or standing, as long as he is looking up. Hold the treat up and say his name to attract his attention. At the same time, give the "heel" hand signal (p.143). Move forward.

3 ▽

Reward at once

Take just one step forward with your puppy moving next to you. Then quickly bring your hand down to deliver the treat, and praise him enthusiastically. This will teach him that he is in the correct place and is doing the right thing by following you.

4 ▷

Take more steps

Gradually increase the number of steps you take before rewarding your puppy. At the start of each new training session, go back to taking just one step before rewarding him, to help him get it right. Then increase the number of steps a little faster.

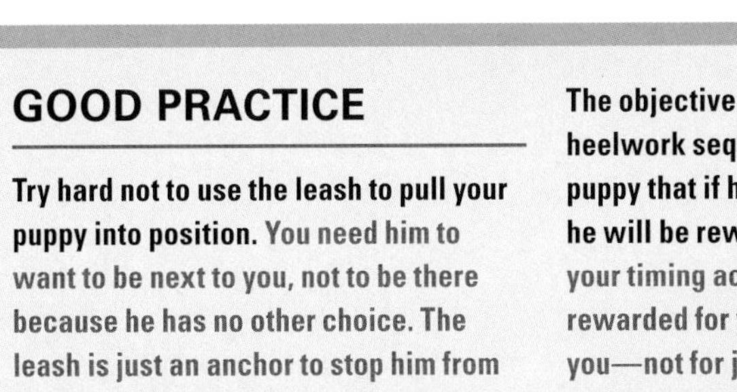

GOOD PRACTICE

Try hard not to use the leash to pull your puppy into position. You need him to want to be next to you, not to be there because he has no other choice. The leash is just an anchor to stop him from running off. In a secure backyard, you can dispense with the leash. This will make the exercise easier since you will have fewer elements to coordinate.

The objective for this part of the heelwork sequence is to teach your puppy that if he walks next to your leg he will be rewarded. Be sure to make your timing accurate, so that he is only rewarded for walking nicely beside you—not for jumping up. Keep practicing until your puppy will go easily into position with the offer of a treat, and will remain there in expectation of a reward while you move in different directions.

No reward
Holding the treat too low will encourage your puppy to jump up to get it. Try holding it higher, well out of reach.

Walking on a **loose leash 2**

Once you have taught your puppy to enjoy walking close to you on one side (pp.158–9), the next step is to teach him not to pull on the leash and to try actively to keep the leash loose at all times.

Once your puppy is happily walking beside you in many different places and with distractions going on around you, teach him to work at keeping the leash loose rather than pulling it. It will be easier to teach him if you choose a time when he is well exercised and tired, rather than when he is full of energy. Be consistent with your training so your puppy learns that pulling is unrewarding.

1 ◁

Pulling ahead

If your puppy forges ahead on a walk, watch the leash carefully and get ready to stop the instant it tightens. Hold the lead against your middle to help you do this, especially if your puppy is large and strong.

2 △

Stop and wait

Abruptly stop as the leash goes tight, preventing your puppy from making any further forward progress. Your aim is to teach him that when he tightens the leash, all forward motion stops, which is the opposite of what he expects.

3 ▽

Bring him back

Lure your puppy back to your side with a treat, reward him for being in the right position, and start again. Over time and with many repetitions, your puppy will begin to learn that it is not worth trying to pull ahead.

4 △

Active walking

Be consistent and stop every time your puppy pulls. He will actively try to keep the leash loose so he doesn't have to stop. When he begins to walk nicely alongside you, relax your hands down beside you.

GOOD PRACTICE

If you can, begin teaching heelwork from the moment you put your puppy on the leash, practicing in the house and yard before taking him out on walks. As with so many training and behavior problems, if he never learns the bad habit of pulling during puppyhood, he will not do it when he is an adult.

It takes time and patience to achieve good loose-leash walking. But if you put the time in while your puppy is still young, your efforts will be amply rewarded later, with an adult dog that doesn't pull on his leash. It is also much easier to teach puppies when they are young, since they walk more slowly. Even so, this technique will also work for older puppies, provided you have plenty of time and patience.

As with all exercises, practice walking on a loose leash in one place to begin with, then in different places, and finally with gradually increasing distractions going on around you.

Easy walking
Walking with a dog that keeps the leash loose is a pleasure that both of you can enjoy.

Come close
When walking past other people, ask your puppy to come to heel to keep him out of their way.

Retrieve

The retrieve exercise forms the basis of many other enjoyable activities for your puppy. It allows you to get the toy back after chase games, and is a useful way to use up excess energy and keep him out of trouble.

Begin with easy retrieves with your puppy's favorite toy. Teach him how to retrieve over several sessions, paying particular attention to stage 4, so that your puppy learns to enjoy coming back to you.

Later, you can work on teaching him to pick up belongings other than toys, fetch non-moving items, and place an object in your hand after retrieving it (pp.166–7).

1 ▽

Building enthusiasm
Before throwing the toy, excite your puppy with the thought of taking it from you. Move it rapidly and erratically in front of him until he is thoroughly stimulated.

2 ▷

Throw the toy
While your puppy is watching, throw the toy in a straight line or low arc just a few yards away. Enjoy watching your puppy run after the toy and pounce on it. Keep quiet as he does so.

"Fetch!"

3 △

Coming back

As soon as your puppy has the toy in his mouth, walk or run backward, being careful not to fall down. At the same time, slap your thighs and encourage him with your voice to run back to you.

4 ▷

Give lots of praise

When your puppy reaches you, rub his body gently and praise him in an excited tone. Be careful not to put your hands near his head or mouth, or he will think you are trying to take the toy.

GOOD PRACTICE

Once you have taught your puppy to run back to you with the toy in his mouth for lavish praise and attention, wait until he begins to get bored with holding it. You will notice his jaw beginning to relax and his head dropping. At this point, offer him a tasty treat with one hand, while holding the other below his mouth to catch the toy.

You also need to teach your puppy the voice cue "Fetch!" once he is retrieving regularly. Give this verbal command just before you throw the toy so he learns to associate it with grabbing the object.

Practice at home until he brings back the toy every time. Once he is reliable, teach him to retrieve toys on walks, in quiet areas at first, and then with increasing distractions, until he will play anywhere.

Toy retrieval
Try not to let your puppy see you reaching for his toy. Instead, offer him the treat first. Catch the toy with the other hand as he opens his mouth to take the treat.

Fetching for fun
Play, and the interaction with owners it brings, can be a powerful reward for older puppies if they are taught to enjoy playing with toys and learn to retrieve them from an early age.

Developing the **retrieve**

Once you have taught the basic retrieve (pp.162–3), you can develop it until your puppy will pick up any object and return it, and will wait for your cue before retrieving something.

Make sure your puppy has learned to retrieve toys really well before you progress. These advanced exercises help your puppy learn self-control, and make him really useful to have around, since he will pick up any indicated item and put it in your hand. Building on these skills, you can then teach him the chase recall (pp.170–1).

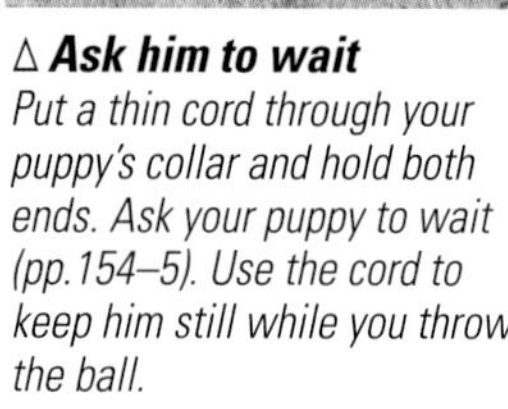

△ ***Ask him to wait***
Put a thin cord through your puppy's collar and hold both ends. Ask your puppy to wait (pp.154–5). Use the cord to keep him still while you throw the ball.

△ ***Stationary objects***
Excite your puppy with an object before throwing it. Hold him back until the object has been stationary for a few seconds. Then send him to fetch it. If he has lost interest, try again, releasing him sooner this time.

▷ ***"Fetch!"***
Make your puppy wait until he settles. Then ask him to fetch the ball, releasing one end of the cord so it flows through his collar as he takes off.

"**Retrieving** is a **useful skill** to **teach** your puppy, since many **games and activities rely on it.**"

△ ***Pick it up***
If your puppy drops the ball on his way to you, encourage him to fetch again, pointing to it and making encouraging noises. If he is no longer interested, push the ball to make it roll away and revive his interest.

▷ ***Deliver to hand***
While your puppy is running toward you, lower your hand ready to catch the ball, and ask him to "drop" (p.143). If he drops too soon, encourage him to pick it up again before trying a second time.

GOOD PRACTICE

Retrieving is a useful skill to teach, since many games and other activities rely on it. You need to have taught your puppy to retrieve competently before teaching games such as finding hidden objects (pp.180–1) or taking messages to people (pp.184–5).

Once your puppy fetches items on cue, you can ask him to do tasks around the house, such as pick up something you have dropped. Performing such tasks for rewards and praise from you gives him a job to do, uses up his energy, and raises his self-esteem. He will enjoy it and you will have a willing helper.

Gradually ask your puppy to pick up items that resemble his toys less and less. Metal objects, or those that dangle when carried, are hard to pick up and hold, so save those for later training. You can also teach him to hold an object while walking beside you, by praising him when he does so and encouraging him to pick it up if he drops it.

Fetch the keys
Your puppy may find it hard to pick up hard items, such as your keys, so use a soft toy key-ring to help him to do it, and give him plenty of encouragement.

Sit at a **distance**

Training your puppy to sit at a distance enables you to stop him wherever he is. This can be extremely useful in an emergency when you need to stop him urgently to keep him out of danger.

This is an advanced exercise, so only tackle it once your puppy already completely understands a number of cues—especially how to sit in response to a hand signal (pp.148–9). Once your puppy knows the cue for sitting when he is stationary, you can teach him to stop and sit in a situation where he is running around. You can also teach your puppy to lie down at a distance in the same way.

1 ◁

Up close

Stand close to your puppy and ask a friend to hold his collar, so that he gets used to having someone beside him. Ask your puppy to sit in the usual way, using a clear hand signal (p.143).

2 △

Reward him

Give your puppy a treat when he sits. Repeat stages 1 and 2 several times. He cannot move closer to you now, but may try to later—he has learned that the cue means "Sit right in front of me and you will be rewarded."

3 ▽

Move farther away

Take a step back and give the hand signal for "sit." Your friend must gently restrain your puppy from moving forward. Ask him to sit again. If he does not understand, your assistant should lure him into a sit, but not feed him.

"Sit!"

4

Run forward

As soon as your puppy sits, run forward to give him a treat. Always go to him with the reward, so that he learns to wait for it. Repeat until he is sitting at a distance when you give the cue.

GOOD PRACTICE

Once your puppy is sitting at a distance in lots of different places with your friend ready to stop him moving forward, teach him again from the beginning without someone restraining him. Help your puppy to get it right by moving away gradually. If this is difficult, you may need to do more work with a friend helping out first.

When your puppy is sitting readily at a distance, begin to teach him to stop and sit when he is on the move. At first, ask him to sit just as he is coming to a natural stop. Then, gradually, make it more difficult by asking him to sit when he is moving at faster speeds.

Emergency stop
Being able to stop your puppy and get him to sit at a distance could prevent injury or even save his life.

Chase recall

Being able to recall your puppy from a chase is vital if you want him to be under complete control and safe when off the leash. Begin by teaching him a chase recall using toys, and progress to other things he may chase.

This exercise is an important lesson for all puppies, and especially for breeds in which the chase instinct is strong. Teaching the chase recall with toys gives you the foundation of this exercise. You can then progress to practicing in real-life situations, near things your puppy is likely to chase, to ensure that you have complete control when you really need it.

1 △
Creating enthusiasm
Excite your puppy with a toy, and pretend to throw it in front of you. When he turns to see where it is, turn and throw the toy behind you.

2 △
Stop him running
As your puppy turns and runs toward the toy, stop him by stepping forward to stand in his way, and hold out your hand in a "wait" signal (p.143).

"As **your puppy** turns and runs toward the toy**, stop him** by **standing in his way.**"

Better toy
As soon as your puppy has stopped in front of you, distract him from the first toy by showing him a toy he prefers.

4

Chase
Throw the second toy in front of you, in the opposite direction of the first toy, for your puppy to chase. Pick up the first toy yourself.

GOOD PRACTICE

Only stop your puppy running after the toy once in every five throws at random. If you stop him more than this, he will become hesitant about running out after the ball and you will begin to lose his enthusiasm.

Don't run your puppy to the point of exhaustion. Up to 20 chases are enough for one session, depending on the fitness level of your puppy and how warm the weather is. Because you can stop him only four times in twenty chases, the opportunities to learn the chase recall are limited, so be patient and keep practicing until your puppy learns what he has to do.

Remember to begin teaching this exercise in a quiet location with no distractions. As your puppy learns the concept of the chase recall, you can progress to training him in places that offer more distractions, where he will find it more difficult to concentrate.

Real-life training
Once your puppy has learned the chase recall, teach him to ignore other moving objects, such as bicycles or joggers. Use a training line to keep him safe, and teach him to come to you for chase games with toys instead as they go past.

Fun stuff

Once you have mastered the basics, it is time to **have some fun**. Teaching your puppy the exercises in this section will **amuse you both**, and others, and is certainly **worth the effort**. With **positive training**, dogs love to **show off** and **gain approval from an audience**; they also love the chance to **earn treats** or play a game with their favorite toy. These activities help to keep them **mentally stimulated**, give them a **role to perform**—that of entertainer—and **increase their self-esteem**. Puppies never forget exercises they learn when they are very young, so if you take the **time to teach your puppy now**, you will **have fun together for years to come**.

SMART PUPPY
Teaching your puppy tricks will help to use up excess energy and keep him busy—and your friends will be impressed by his talents.

Wave and **hi-five**

The wave is an easy trick to teach your puppy, and you can develop it later into the hi-five. The two exercises make a good beginning and end to a sequence of tricks if you want to put some together for a display.

The wave has the same beginning as the hi-five. Teach the wave first and make sure your puppy knows it well before attempting to teach him the hi-five. Keep sessions short and take it slowly.

Practice the wave in one place first, returning every time for successive sessions, until your puppy has learned the trick thoroughly. Then teach in other places around the house and in the garden.

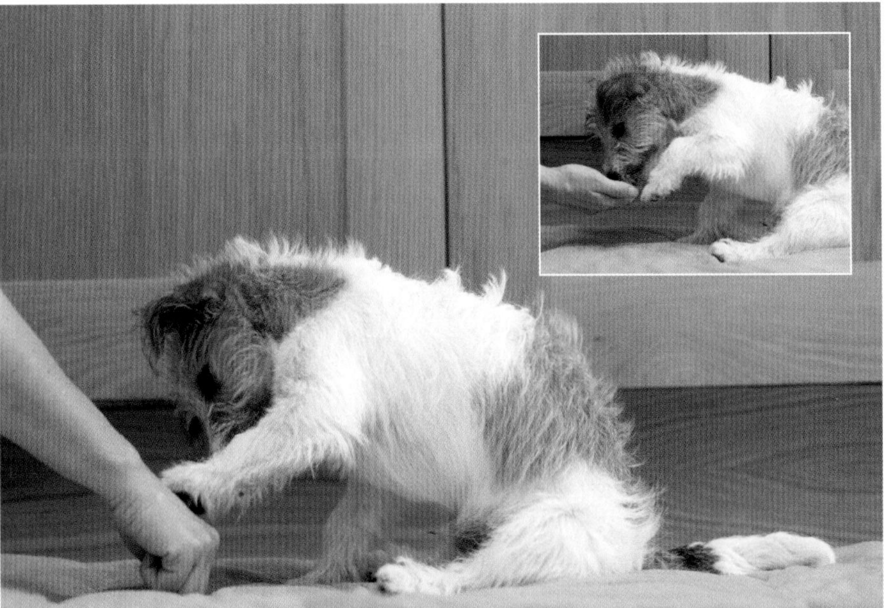

1

Learning to paw

Wrap your hand around a smelly treat, and place your hand on the ground. Wait until your puppy moves his paw toward it. Open your hand instantly to reveal the treat and reward him. Continue over several sessions, until he has learned to paw at your hand.

Lifting higher

Slowly lift your hand higher over several sessions, instantly rewarding your puppy with a treat when he paws at your hand. Introduce your hand signal, giving it just before you offer the hand holding the treat, so that he learns to associate the cue with the action.

"Hi-five!"

Waving

This exercise becomes more difficult once you have lifted your hand higher and your puppy can no longer touch your hand. Watch closely for any movement of his paw and reward instantly. Be patient and reward good attempts, and he will gradually learn to do a full wave.

Doing the hi-five

Once your puppy has learned how to wave confidently and in different situations, you can turn the action into a hi-five. Stretch out your hand, so that as he lowers his paw, it comes to rest against your palm. Reward him immediately with a treat.

"**First** teach **your puppy** the **wave,** and make sure he has **learned it thoroughly** before you attempt to teach him the **hi-five.**"

GOOD PRACTICE

Once your hand moves too high for your puppy to reach easily, you may find that he jumps up to put his paw on your hand. Ignore this and ask him to sit, then wave again. Watch carefully for any small movement of his paw and instantly reward this to tell him he was right. If he doesn't understand, lower your hand to show him what he needs to do. He should then repeat the action when you raise your hand again.

When your puppy manages to perform a hi-five and touches your hand with his paw, make sure that you lightly support the paw. Do not try to grasp it, because this may make him withdraw it—some dogs find it threatening to have their paw held.

While your puppy is learning the wave and hi-five, kneel down or crouch. Once he understands the commands, you can teach him to do the tricks with you standing up.

Roll over and play dead

This is a useful exercise for occasions when you need to look underneath your puppy for a health check or for grooming. You can also develop rolling over into a funny trick to show your friends.

Only teach this exercise once your puppy is reliably lying down on command (pp.152–3). Your puppy needs to feel safe to roll over, so choose a place with a soft surface where he feels comfortable, away from other dogs or any disturbance. Once he understands the roll-over position and will go into it with a treat to reward him, introduce the hand signal, and teach it in different places and with distractions.

1.

Head sideways

Holding a tempting treat to your puppy's nose, slowly lure his head around to the side. Position your hand so that you can move it farther when you progress to stage 2. Allow him to lick and chew small pieces off the treat to keep him interested.

2.

Lure his head back

Gradually lure your puppy's head around and back. This is difficult, so be patient. Keep the treat level with your puppy's nose, since he will stand up if it goes too high. Feed the treat to reward him and repeat.

GOOD PRACTICE

Be patient. The luring takes time for you both to learn. Try to position your hand in such a way that, if your puppy's head follows it, he will end up in the right position. If you feel frustrated, reward his best try and end the session.

Praise your puppy calmly while he is in position, rewarding him with a few treats at first. Too much excited praise will encourage him to get up.

Stop rewarding as soon as he moves so that he learns it is worth staying down. Let him know the exercise is over with a word cue, such as "Finished!"

Play dead!
Progress to teaching your puppy to collapse from standing into a down and roll. Once he has learned the action, teach him a hand signal.

3 ◁ △

Rolling for a reward

Keep everything calm and, after several attempts, your puppy should relax enough to roll on to his side and, eventually, on to his back. Feed him treats in this position and reward him with calm praise to let him know this is what you wanted.

4

Use a hand signal

Once your puppy is responding reliably every time and can easily follow the lure, begin to turn your hand movement into a cue. Hold your hand out in a clear signal. Exaggerate your hand signal at first so that he learns to anticipate what is required.

No threat here
Puppies often roll over to display their undersides if they are feeling overwhelmed by a person or another dog. They also roll on to their backs when relaxing, for fun, or to gain attention.

Find the **toy**

Finding a hidden toy is a great way to use up your puppy's excess energy without exhausting yourself. Once he has learned how to play the game, you can hide toys or treats all over the house and send him to find them.

Begin with your puppy's favorite toy and gradually progress to using other objects. If he is reluctant to look for soft toys, try using rubber toys or small boxes that can be stuffed with food. Start slowly, leaving toys around the room and helping him to find them by pointing to the hiding place. Gradually reduce the amount of help you give and progress to hiding toys in other rooms.

1 ◁

Build his excitement
Create motivation for the search by playing with your puppy's favorite toy, teasing him with it, and moving it around so that he really wants it. Once he is excited, quickly hide the toy under a cushion.

"Find it!"

2 ▷

Start the search
After letting your puppy see where the toy is, take him just out of sight and quickly send him to find it. Give him plenty of encouragement and point to the hiding place as a visual signal. Help him to find the toy if you need to.

"Good boy!"

3 ◁

Praise gently

Allow your puppy to take the toy and let him know how smart he is. Praise him verbally, and reward him with gentle stroking on his sides and back. Avoid his head and the toy, so that he doesn't think you are trying to take it from him.

4 ▽

Extend the search

Once your puppy has learned to find his toy wherever it is in the room, begin to hide it in other rooms. Teach him to find different toys, too, and go on to hide multiple items.

GOOD PRACTICE

Your puppy needs to learn to use his nose to find the object, so choose soft, old toys at first rather than hard, new ones.

Make it easy for your puppy to learn to search, encouraging him and showing him where to find things at first. Make it a little more difficult each time.

Leave the toy with your puppy for a while after he has found it, as a reward for all his hard work. Taking the toy away too soon may make future efforts to hunt for toys seem futile.

Some puppies are less interested than others in owning toys and find the game of finding a hidden object unrewarding to play alone. Such puppies need constant encouragement from their owners to do the work necessary to find the toy. If your puppy doesn't seem to grasp the point of the game, make it really easy and put toys in obvious places.

Contented dog
Hide-and-seek games will quickly tire out your puppy. Afterward, he will feel good and be content to lie down and rest.

Crawl

Crawling is a fun trick to teach your puppy. Once he has learned to crawl well, try using a low jump as a prop. Your puppy can amuse his audience by crawling under the pole rather than jumping over it.

Teaching your puppy to crawl is easy. However, it needs lots of repetition for him to understand that he needs to keep his rear end low, rather than crawling with his front feet and hopping with his back legs. Start on a soft carpet until he knows what to do and has learned to respond on cue, then repeat the exercise in different places and on different surfaces until he can crawl anywhere.

1 ◁

Slowly move the treat
Your puppy needs to know how to lie down on cue (pp.152–3) before he can learn to crawl. Ask him to lie down, and put a treat close to his nose. Gradually move the treat away. Keep it low and move it really slowly so that he has time to follow it. Watch for movement in his legs.

2 ▷

Reward effort
Give your puppy part of the treat when one paw moves forward. Repeat, rewarding him whenever a paw advances. When he has moved all four paws, reward him well. Repeat stages 1 and 2, gradually asking for more each time before rewarding, until your puppy will crawl readily after the lure.

"**Do not ask** for **too much, too soon** from your puppy. **Keep sessions short** and **successful.**"

3 ◁

Hand signal

After many sessions, when your puppy is easily crawling after the lure, ask him to do a few short crawls and reward him with a tasty treat. Next time, move your hand away from him in a hand signal, then reward him with a treat if he crawls. If he doesn't, go back to luring and try again later.

4 △

Reward success

When your puppy crawls in response to your hand signal, being careful to keep his rear end low, reward him with a treat and generous praise. Crawling is not a natural movement, so keep your training sessions short to avoid tiring him.

GOOD PRACTICE

If your puppy's rear end comes up as he tries to crawl, do not reward him. Don't scold him, just wait until his rear end sinks down again and reward. Raising his back legs to push himself along is the natural thing to do, so wait patiently until he learns another way to move.

Do not ask for too much, too soon from your puppy. Crawling takes a lot of energy and uses different muscles compared to ordinary walking, so keep sessions short and successful.

Keep the treat close to your puppy's nose, so that he can lick and chew at it, slowly feeding more through your fingers as he nibbles. Move the treat away really slowly until he has learned the action you require. If you get too far ahead, he will be tempted to stand up and walk forward to reach the treat.

Take it outside

Once your puppy can crawl on cue, teach him in different places, including outside, then with distractions until he will do it anywhere.

Take a message

This exercise is fun and useful, and dogs love the social interaction it brings. You can eventually teach your puppy to find a named person and deliver a message wherever they are in the house or yard.

Make sure your puppy can do the retrieve with different objects as well as toys (pp.166–7) really well before you try this exercise. Once you have taught the basics using the stages below, teach him to take the message to a named person, adding their name at stage 1, and repeating often until your puppy has learned the cue. Begin with the person in sight, then move them slowly farther away.

1 ◁

Excite him
Play with a piece of paper to get your puppy excited about holding it. When he has it in his mouth, turn him toward your friend and ask him to "take it."

2 ▽

Give the message
As soon as you have asked your puppy to take the message, your friend should call his name and give the "come" hand signal (p.143). Point and encourage him to go to her as she calls him.

GOOD PRACTICE

Only ask friends to help you once your puppy is fetching the note from the floor and returning it to your hand for a treat. Otherwise you will waste their time.

If your puppy is struggling to find people in another room, do more practice while they are in sight, then slowly move them behind the door, and then farther away.

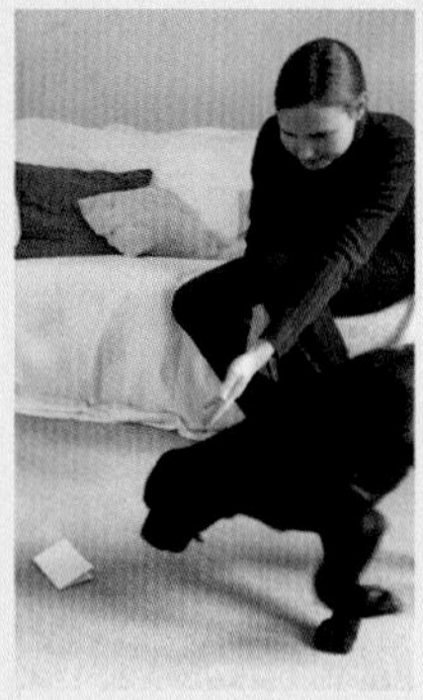

Fetch it
If your puppy drops the note before delivering it, encourage him to pick it up, using an excited voice and pointing to where it is lying on the floor. Once he has the message back in his mouth, send him to your friend, and ask her to call.

Here it is
Once your puppy has learned that he will get treats for delivering the note, he will be happy to present it to the recipient. Until then, ask your friend to gently praise him and stroke his sides, taking the note when he is bored with holding it.

3

Praise him

When your puppy arrives, your friend should praise him warmly, stroking along his body, but avoiding the head. Eventually, as the excitement subsides, ask your friend to take the paper from your puppy and reward him well with a tasty treat.

Index

E

F

G

H

I

J

Glossary

ACTION
The movement a puppy has to make in order to be rewarded.

ADOLESCENT CHEWING
The second stage of chewing, which occurs during adolescence, when a puppy is approximately 7–10 months of age.

BREED
A grouping of pure-bred dogs that share a clearly defined set of characteristics.

COUNTER-CONDITIONING
Pairing a previously frightening stimulus at low intensity—such as distant traffic—with rewards to change the puppy's view of the stimulus to a positive one.

CROSSBREED
The offspring of pure-bred parents of two different breeds.

CUE
A signal used to indicate that a puppy should perform an action—either a hand signal or a voice cue.

DESENSITIZATION
Reducing fear of a noise, a place, or an object, through repeated exposures of gradually increasing intensity—similar to habituation.

HABITUATION
Getting used to the non-living part of the human world—for example, washing machines or vacuum cleaners—through gradual but repeated exposure.

HAND SIGNAL
A type of cue; using one or both hands to form a unique signal that becomes associated with a particular action—the puppy learns that when the signal is given, rewards are available for doing that action.

HEELWORK
Training a puppy to walk beside you, either off or on the leash.

HIERARCHY OF REWARDS
Rewards are graded from most liked to least favorite, and given according to the difficulty of the action required.

HOUSEBREAKING
Teaching your puppy to go to the bathroom in an appropriate place, usually outside of the house.

HOUSE LINE
A length of line without a handle that can be attached to a puppy's collar when you are in the house—this allows you to stop unwanted behaviors, such as chasing.

INBREEDING
Breeding from closely related individuals, usually over several generations.

JACKPOT
A selection of high-value rewards, made up of both food and games, given at random to celebrate a good performance.

LATENT LEARNING
The subconscious learning that seems to take place in between training sessions, when your puppy is resting or sleeping.

LURING
Moving a piece of food in a particular direction so that your puppy follows it into the position you require.

MONGREL
A dog of mixed or unknown breeding.

NEUTERING
Removal of the male or female reproductive organs under anesthetic.

PEDIGREE
Recorded ancestry of a pure-bred animal.

PLAY BITING
The way in which a puppy learns to play with his littermates—this behavior should be directed toward toys, rather than humans, from a young age.

POSITIVE TRAINING
Method based on rewarding good behavior in order to teach successful responses to cues.

PUBERTY
A developmental stage which occurs at approximately 6 months of age, when puppies become mentally and physically ready for reproduction.

PUPPY CHEWING
The first stage of chewing, this occurs when the puppy teeth begin to fall out, at around 4–5 months of age.

PUPPY MILL
A place that breeds large numbers of puppies indiscriminately and for financial gain, without considering the health and temperament of the puppies or the welfare of the parent animals.

PUPPY PARTY
An occasion for very young puppies to meet one another in a controlled environment, usually in a veterinarian's office or similar place.

PUPPY PLAYPEN
An enclosed area with bedding and newspaper, enabling your puppy to leave the nest to go to the bathroom if he is left too long. It can be used to contain your puppy when you are not able to supervise him, or left open as a place to rest.

PUPPY TEETH
Small, pointed teeth that begin to fall out after 4–5 months and are replaced by larger, less sharp, permanent teeth.

REWARD
Something that your puppy really wants—usually food-based, but can be a toy or a game, or freedom—that can be given in return for good behavior.

SELECTIVE BREEDING
Controlled breeding of carefully chosen individuals in order to retain desirable characteristics in the offspring, and remove undesirable ones.

SHAPING
Rewarding small movements toward an eventual goal or action.

SOCIALIZATION
Introducing young puppies to new people, other dogs, and other animals, so that they learn to adopt a friendly approach in all future new situations.

STRIPPING
The removal by hand of old hair from a wire-haired coat.

TARGETING
Teaching a puppy over several sessions to touch a target with either his nose or paw, then moving the target to different places—so you can teach him to close a door or press a pedal, for example.

TOPCOAT
Coat of long, heavy, guard hairs.

UNDERCOAT
The dense, usually short, soft coat closest to the skin.

VOICE CUE
A word spoken to indicate that a reward is available if the puppy carries out a particular action.

Contacts

DOG AND PUPPY TRAINING

Dog and puppy training classes, or individual tuition, can help you to progress more rapidly and assist with any individual difficulties. Choose someone experienced and knowledgeable, who uses only positive methods with both dogs and their owners. Other good sources of information about local trainers are local vets, dog wardens, groomers, and pet stores.

The following are useful organizations to contact when looking for a dog or puppy trainer:

USA AND CANADA

National Association of Dog Obedience Instructors
www.nadoi.org
Tel: 505-890-5957
PO Box 1439, Socorro, NM 87801

The Association of Pet Dog Trainers
www.apdt.com
Email: information@apdt.com
Tel: 1-800-738-3647
101 North Main Street, Suite 610,
Greenville, SC 29601

The Canadian Association of Professional Pet Dog Trainers
www.cappdt.ca/public/jpage/1/p/Home/content.do
Email: secretary@cappdt.ca
CAPPDT
c/o Patricia Robertson, Secretary
2106 McCracken's Landing Road, RR #2,
Lakefield, ON K0L 2H0, Canada

BEHAVIOR PROBLEMS

If you are experiencing behavior problems with your puppy, it is best to get help fast before habits become too established. Look for someone with both practical experience and academic knowledge. They should work on veterinary referral, and be insured.

Contact the following organizations or ask your veterinarian to refer you to someone they trust:

USA AND CANADA

Animal Behavior Society
http://animalbehaviorsociety.org

The International Association of Animal Behavior Consultants
www.iaabc.org
Tel: 484-843-1091
565 Callery Road, Cranberry Township,
PA 16066

SOURCES OF NEW DOGS AND PUPPIES

As well as breeders, reputable rescue organizations are a good source of new puppies and adult dogs. Try to find a center where they make the effort to assess all the dogs in their care so you can choose one to suit your temperament and lifestyle. The following are useful organizations to contact when looking for a new puppy:

USA AND CANADA

American Society for the Prevention of Cruelty to Animals
www.aspca.org
Tel: 212-876-7700
424 E. 92nd Street, New York, NY
10128-6804

Canadian Society for the Prevention of Cruelty to Animals
www.canadianspca.com
Email: admin@ canadianspca.com
Tel: 514-735-2711 ext. 2240
5215 West Jean-Talon,
Montreal QC H4P 1X4
Canada

Humane Society of Canada
www.humanesociety.com
Email: michael@humanesociety.com
Tel: 1-800-641-Kind
1500 West Georgia St., Suite 1555
PO Box 62, Vancouver, BC V6G 2Z6
Canada

Humane Society of the United States
www.hsus.org
Tel: 202-452-1100
2100 L Street, NW Washington, DC 20037

For further information on breeders with puppies, contact:
American Kennel Club
www.akc.org
Tel: 919-233-9767
8051 Arco Corporate Drive, Suite 100,
Raleigh, NC 27617-3390

Canadian Kennel Club
www.ckc.ca
Email: information@ckc.ca
Tel: 416-675-5511
200 Ronson Drive, Suite 400,
Etobicoke, Ontario M9W 5Z9
Canada

Acknowledgments

The author would like to thank the following: All the owners and puppies who appear in this book, together with Rachel Butler, Beverley Courtney, and Bobs Broadbent, who provided invaluable assistance with the photo shoots. A very big thank you also goes to Victoria Wiggins, Project Editor, who was a pleasure to work with, despite the very difficult task of extracting a book from deep within the recesses of my thoughts and breathing life into it on paper.

Dorling Kindersley would like to thank the following:
For additional editorial: Jamie Ambrose, Anna Fischel

Also, Rachel Butler, Bobs Broadbent, and Beverley Courtney, Tima Lund and her litter of puppies, Valley Veterinary Group, Vets on the Park, and the staff and dogs at Battersea Dogs and Cats Home, Old Windsor Branch.

And those who modeled in the book: Samantha Arrowsmith, Gwen Bailey, Mitun Banerjee, Jennifer Barker, Keith Bishop, Lucinda Bishop, Gillian Blythe, Kristina Bobs, Ramie Booth, Chris Bowley, Rachael Bowley, Caroline Bradley, Bobs Broadbent, Robert Bromley, Helen Buckley, Rachel Butler, Keith Cattell, Jeremy Clarke, Neil Clarke, Sophie Clarke, Edward Coles, Sue Collier, Peter Connor, Beverley Courtney, Graham Currie, Heide Cussell, Louise Daly, Sarah Davies, Helen Davis, David Dixey, Jackie Dixey, Sarah Dray, Gary Dunning, Sumer Eaglestone, Paul Evans, Emily Fincham, Pam Fisher, Vic Fisher, Michelle Fittus, Jo Freegard, Jo Goodenough, Rosemarie Griffiths, Marie Harrison, James Haslam, Amaya Herold, David Herold, Lorna Herold, Poppy Herold, Willow Herold, Dylan Hill, Josh Hill, Lewis Hill, Tracy Hill, Peter Hobson, Alan Hocknell, Richard Horsford, John Howson, Shellee Illingworth, Lee Jackson-Horn, Jan Jones, Jo Jones, Natasha Jones, Tanya Jones, Steve Jones, Zac Jones, Sue Lim, Tima Lund, Carla Mann, Alice Martineau, Ali Masters, Isabel Masters, Stephen Masters, Hilary McLaughlin, Samuel McSweeney, Karen Miles, Niall Minihane, Catrin Osborn, Graham Ostridge, Caroline Pincott, Donna Richards, Margaret Scules, James Scull, Jill Scull, Lucy Scull, James Self, Jasmine Self, Dominic Shaw, Vicky Short, Nina Sjoberg, Fenny Sukimto, Emma Taylor, Laura Thomas, Carys Thurlby, Annette Watts, Archie Watts, Helen Weston, Victoria Wiggins, Jennifer Woodford, Perdita Woodley, Vanessa Woodley, Nigel Wright, Christine Young

Thank you to all the puppies and dogs whose photographs appear in this book:
Alfie, Angus, Archie, Bailey, Baxter, Ben, Benny, Bess, Betty Boo, Blade, Blanche, Boris, Boysie, Bracken, Brian, Buddy, Buster, Buttons, Charlie, Chesil, Dexter, Dixie, Dora, Eddie, Elsa, Faolan, Fly, Guinness, Jess, Lenny, Lilah, Lottie, Maggie, Molly, Monty, Murphy, Otto, Pebbles, Pepper, Rocky, Ruby, Quinn, Rufus, Scrappy, Scrumpy, Spider, Stan, Stanley, Tai, Tia-Diki, Tory, Walter, Yorkie, Zach

Picture credits

The publisher would like to thank the following for their kind permission to reproduce their photographs:
l=left, r=right, t=top, c=center, a=above, b=below.

10-11 Photolibrary: Peter Thompson (l). **13 Corbis:** Don Mason/Blend Images. **14 Alamy Images:** David Crossland (br). **15 Alamy Images:** Richard Sheppard (tr). **Fotolia:** lunamarina (b). **22 Corbis:** Pat Doyle (bl). **23 Alamy Images:** Waldemar Dabrowski (tr); Paul Springett 01 (bl). **24 Alamy Images:** Life on white (bl). **Corbis:** Pat Doyle (br); Yoshihisa Fujita/MottoPet/amanaimages (tl). **naturepl.com:** Artlist International (tr). **25 Alamy Images:** Petra Wegner (br). **26 Alamy Images:** imagebroker (bl); Juniors Bildarchiv (br). **Corbis:** Rubberball (c). **naturepl.com:** Artlist International (cl). **27 Alamy Images:** imagebroker (tr); Tom Viggars (c). **28 Corbis:** Pat Doyle (bl). **30 Corbis:** Yoshihisa Fujita/MottoPet/amanaimages (bl); Gyro Photography/amanaimages (br). **31 Alamy Images:** Petra Wegner (tc). **Animal Photography:** Sally Anne Thompson (bc). **Corbis:** Yoshihisa Fujita/MottoPet/amanaimages (br). Getty Images: MIXA (cr). **34 Alamy Images:** Petra Wegner (tl). **Animal Photography:** Sally Anne Thompson (bl). **Corbis:** Michael Kloth (cr). **35 Corbis:** Pat Doyle (br); Peter M. Fisher (bl). **36 Corbis:** Kevin Oke/All Canada Photos (crb). **37 Alamy Images:** Waldemar Dabrowski (cl); Juniors Bildarchiv (clb). **Corbis:** Michael Kloth (crb). **38 Alamy Images:** Juniors Bildarchiv (bc). **Kennel Club:** Farlap (cl). **39 Alamy Images:** Juniors Bildarchiv (c). **Kennel Club:** Farlap (bl). **40 Alamy Images:** Juniors Bildarchiv (cl). **Kennel Club:** Allen Parton (bl). **42 Alamy Images:** Juniors Bildarchiv (cl). **naturepl.com:** Mark Taylor (cra). **43 Alamy Images:** Juniors Bildarchiv (tr); Tierfotoagentur (br). **44 Alamy Images:** Tierfotoagentur (bc). Cory Pulliam: (br). **45 Alamy Images:** Compix (tr); Life on white (br). **Corbis:** DLILLC (bl). **Kennel Club:** Diane Pearce (tl). **46 Alamy Images:** Nick Baylis (tr); Petra Wegner (bc); Tierfotoagentur (br). **47 Alamy Images:** Paul Cotney (bl). **Corbis:** Michael Kloth (br). **Getty Images:** Nicki Pardo (cra)

Note

Every effort has been made to ensure that the information in this book is accurate. Neither the publishers nor the author accept any legal responsibility for any personal injury or injuries to dogs, or other damage or loss arising from the undertaking of any of the activities or exercises presented in this book, or from the reliance on any advice in this book. If your dog is sick or has behavioral problems, please seek the advice of a qualified professional, such as a vet or behavioral expert.